## Praise for *Leadership Actually*

"*Leadership Actually* is a deceptively simple book that shines a light on this often treacherous and always profound journey. Rooted in deep psychological principles, military and business strategy, as well as ancient wisdom, it invites us to reimagine leadership in a holistic, pragmatic, and far more human way in every area of our lives."

—Rob Meekins, cofounder and former CEO, Med School Tutors

"This is a book that delivers on its promise: it teaches leadership in a way that's both insightful and actionable. It's packed with frameworks, practical guidance, and real-world stories that tie everything together. *Leadership Actually* is a valuable read for anyone looking to sharpen their leadership skills or build them from the ground up."

—Quang Do, Partner, RevEng Consulting

"*Leadership Actually* presents a distinctive, experience-based program that uses real-life situations to build leadership skills. Instead of abstract theory, it offers practical, step-by-step guidance on essential tools for leading effectively. Grounded in proven methodologies and designed for the complexities of today's workplace, it helps managers at every level strengthen their craft. Organizations can draw on its clear lessons to develop leaders who are prepared to thrive in today's world."

—David Kinsman, business advisor, Kunming, China

"This excellent book, crafted to engage a variety of learning styles, offers a clear and insightful analysis of leadership as practiced by true masters of the art. Packed with concise, step-by-step frameworks and vivid, compelling storytelling, it illuminates what's possible. It left a lasting impression on me."

—Chan Lai Huat, author and business consultant, Singapore

"As I step into the responsibility of guiding future healthcare professionals, *Leadership Actually* is the resource I didn't know I needed—but now won't be without. Insightful, practical, and refreshingly applicable across disciplines, this book is already a cornerstone in my leadership toolkit. Whether in personal reflection, classroom discussions, or collaborative efforts with colleagues, its lessons and exercises are tools I'll return to time and time again."

—Sara Glass, DMSc, PA-C, Assistant Professor, Physician Assistant Program, Concordia University, St. Paul

"Leadership today is about more than tasks and outcomes—it's about how we approach them and the growth we inspire along the way. This book brings home key points in a clear and practical way. If you want a leadership book that you'll not only finish but actually use, this is the one."

—Allan McKisson, former vice president of human resources

"*Leadership Actually* is the kind of book that makes you stop, reflect, and then actually do things differently. Honest, practical, and full of heart—I highly recommend it."

—Kerri Gentry, MSW, OPC Social & Activity Center, Rochester, Michigan

"This is a book I would construct if I could write like this. I am tracking on all fronts and can't believe the like-minded parallels I am gathering and gleaning from the book. I hope there are more people in leadership roles that can grab ahold of leading this way. I believe the most important piece is collaboration and giving a voice to members of the team."

—Laurence Becker, Owner, RDS Reliable Door Systems

"*Leadership Actually* stands out because it's practical, heartfelt, and narrative-driven. It avoids the trap of being a purely academic framework or a purely inspirational memoir. It blends both. What I admire most is its insistence that leadership is a craft, a discipline worth honing with the same rigor as medicine, law, or engineering."

—Ross Maiwand, Managing Director, Accenture

"It's a good idea to have two copies of *Leadership Actually*: one for the office to share with colleagues and one for home to share with family and friends. Not only will readers who apply the lessons from the book become more engaged, effective, and confident managers and leaders; they'll also be inspired to lead better and more fulfilling lives."

—E. R. Dunn, President, Dunn Group Ltd.

"*Leadership Actually* eloquently uses the narrative of a Vietnam veteran to remind us that true leadership skills are taught not through training but through an openness to what life and those we encounter bring to us. It reminds us that our leadership is not something we have earned by being better than but an honor we have gained by being open to, a burden we carry by caring for, and a responsibility we assume by hoping for a brighter tomorrow."

—Michelle Craven, PhD, school counselor

"*Leadership Actually* is an invitation to cast aside most of what you have been taught about leadership to make room for a new concept—the craft of leadership—and explore its possibilities for transforming you, those you lead, and the world around you."

—R. Tom Lenz, Emeritus Professor of Management, Kelley School of Business, Indiana University

"After reading *Leadership Actually* once, I know I'll be going back through it again taking detailed notes. It was a truly enjoyable read. While I expected it to be insightful, I was pleasantly surprised by how engaging it felt—never like a textbook. I especially appreciated the alternating structure: Jack's real-life experiences in one chapter, followed by the principles behind them in the next."

—Ben Dunn, Sales Manager, Residential and Commercial Property Management Group

"I was introduced to the information and methods in this book almost fifty years ago. I used them effectively in my military and civilian career, and they essentially changed my life and allowed me to be a much better leader. The content of this book is needed just as much, or more, now as it was years ago. The need for effective leadership does not change. I highly recommend *Leadership Actually* to anyone in a leadership position."

—Michael Cruey, US Army, Retired

# LEADERSHIP ACTUALLY

## Working Together Like Your Life and Livelihood Depend on It

# LEADERSHIP ACTUALLY

## Working Together Like Your Life and Livelihood Depend on It

**THE CO-CREATIVE LEADERSHIP ALLIANCE**

**Velorion Press**

Velorion Press
velorionpress.com

ORDERING INFORMATION
Ordering Information
**Quantity sales.** Special discounts are available on quantity purchases by corporations, associations, and others. For details, contact the "Special Sales Department" at the address above.

**Orders by US trade bookstores and wholesalers.** Please contact BCH: (800) 431-1579 or visit www.bookch.com for details.

Printed in the United States of America

Cataloging-in-Publication-Data

Names: The Co-Creative Leadership Alliance, author.
Title: Leadership actually : working together like your life and livelihood depend on it / The Co-Creative Leadership Alliance.
Description: Includes bibliographical references and index. | Denver, CO: Velorion Press, 2026.
Identifiers: LCCN: 2025923675 | ISBN: 978-1-969069-09-3 (paperback) | 978-1-969069-10-9 (ebook)
Subjects: LCSH Leadership. | Management. | BISAC BUSINESS & ECONOMICS / Leadership
Classification: LCC HD57.7 .C63 2026 | DDC 658.4092--dc23

First Edition
29 28 27 26 25 10 9 8 7 6 5 4 3 2 1

Gloria in excelsis Deo

Leadership is the process of getting other people
to move along together with you, and each other,
with competence and full commitment to achieve a goal.

—Elliott Jaques and Stephen D. Clement

# Contents

# Foreword

In my work, learning, as a mode of leadership, has two components. First, the leader is continually learning, willing to be wrong, comfortable with ambiguity, and intuitively agile. Second, to lead organizations, the learning leader imparts the same curiosity to direct reports, groups, and teams. So a learning leader invites their people to share, to collaborate, and to figure things out.

*Leadership Actually* shows you ways to *live* a level of leadership—at which everyone must claim their personal agency to act on the world—that fits the learning leadership mode.

And it starts with an *actual* war story.

US Army officer Jack Barrett is a unique protagonist for a business book. His combat experience and peacetime organizational effectiveness work combine to demonstrate the contrast between command-and-control stoicism and self-awareness-based development.

The military may seem an unlikely setting from which to learn leadership for some. Historically, however, the US military has been ahead of much of the business world in transitioning from old top-down leadership in favor of more strategically effective modes—modes in which everyone is expected to bring a mindful, thinking component and participate together in leadership. The Center for Creative Leadership, where I was first employed, is steeped in elements of this aspect of modern military science.

Much of what Barrett learned about leadership early in his career was a direct outgrowth of his earliest military experiences. In fact, it was within them that the seeds were sown that grew into the idea of *Leadership Actually*. The experiences arose from the need to pay attention and "sweat the details." These behaviors were useful in Barrett's day. They may be even more so for you today.

There's a freshness about this book, both in its concept and in the authors' resource manual for how to achieve it. It deconstructs leadership not just to learn about it and put it back together but instead to reassemble it to be more efficient and more effective. It frames leadership as a craft to be observed, modeled, practiced, and mastered. It goes a step further by describing how you can do those things. Best of all, *Leadership Actually* is human and compassionate.

It's not necessarily easy to write a leadership book that has those qualities.

We are surrounded by big theories, catchy slogans, and endless models, and yet, when the moment comes to lead—in a crisis, in a team meeting, in a simple conversation—the true work of leadership is far more grounded. It is not abstract. It's real because it's lived.

That is why *Leadership Actually* is such an important book. It takes us past the noise and the illusions—the charismatic personas, the shortcuts to influence, the myth of the "born leader"—and leads us back to the heart of what leadership really is: showing up authentically, making sound choices, and creating the conditions for others to thrive.

This is not a dense manual but a book that feels conversational, approachable, and useful. Its stories, frameworks, and tools are not presented as theory for theory's sake; they are meant to be put to work. It is a book that invites reflection but also sparks action. Many who have read it early have described it as "a rare kind of leadership book"—one they not only finished but immediately wanted to use.

The authors remind us that leadership is not about titles or positions. It is not a performance to be staged nor a mask to be worn. Leadership is a practice—sometimes quiet, often demanding, always consequential.

And like any practice, it must be developed, tested, refined, and lived consistently.

As I read *Leadership Actually*, I found myself revisiting my own career and asking the same kinds of reflective questions this book poses to every reader: *What does it mean to lead well, here and now? How am I bringing clarity in a world of confusion? Am I living the example I want others to follow?*

This book does not shy away from the paradoxes of leadership. It acknowledges that leadership today is both harder and more necessary than ever. It insists that the most durable and trustworthy leaders are those who act with integrity, who resist easy answers, and who ground their work in human connection.

For seasoned leaders, *Leadership Actually* will serve as a reset, a reminder of why you chose to lead in the first place. For emerging leaders, it will be a guidebook, urging you to look past superficial success and focus on the deeper craft of leading people well. For consultants, coaches, and educators, it provides language and lessons you can immediately share with those you serve. And for leaders in healthcare, education, business, or the military, it offers a common framework—one that is adaptable, resilient, and deeply human.

Above all, this book is refreshingly real. No jargon. No fads. Just the essence of leadership as it is actually lived, often with courage, humility, and a steady commitment to others.

At a time when the world needs better leaders in every sphere of life, *Leadership Actually* arrives as both a challenge and an invitation to always be learning.

Randall P. White
Principal, Executive Development Group, LLC

# Preface

> Unless someone like you cares a whole awful lot,
> nothing is going to get better. It's not.
>
> —Dr. Seuss

Welcome to *Leadership Actually*. We're delighted you're here! The fact that you are shows that you're one of Dr. Seuss's "someones" who cares deeply about leadership and improving the way you practice it.

We at the Co-Creative Leadership Alliance share that passion, and it's our mission to improve the way leadership is practiced around the world—one leader, one team, and one organization at a time. With this goal in mind, we've distilled the very best of our collective experience into this book to help you lead with skill, confidence, and a deep sense of purpose.

Whether you're leading a team, teaching students, or guiding your family through the labyrinth of daily life, your influence is profound. It can literally help change and heal our troubled world.

## WHY WE WROTE *LEADERSHIP ACTUALLY*

This book is a collective passion project inspired by our years of experience with thousands of leaders, many of whom have been misled or misinformed about the true nature of leadership and how to practice it. Too often, people have been influenced, subtly and otherwise, to model themselves after the tough, stoic, predominantly male figures portrayed in the media, where the human element is routinely treated as an afterthought.

We take a different tack. We approach leadership as a professional craft whose primary purpose goes beyond wielding power or exerting control. Instead, leading others is about helping them unlock their full potential and become active agents in shaping their own futures.

Leadership doesn't happen in isolation; at its best, it's a co-creative process built on robust working relationships, shared experiences, and mutual growth. True leadership is about fostering an environment where people elevate one another—exchanging ideas, skills, and perspectives—to create something greater than any one person could achieve alone.

We'll return to these themes throughout the book, revisiting them from multiple perspectives. As the context shifts, their meaning will evolve and deepen. Each time, we'll uncover new insights and applications—revealing their ongoing relevance to your growth as a leader.

## OUR PREMISE AND GOAL

The book's premise is that leadership has two sides—one illusory and one real (inspired by Joni Mitchell's song "Both Sides Now").

Too often, what many confuse with leadership is a performance rather than a practice, an illusion sustained by charisma, titles, and appearances. Illusory leadership substitutes rhetoric for substance, information for insight, and ego for service.

While this illusion might feel convincing in the moment, it inevitably erodes trust, growth, and collaboration. Beneath the surface, this kind of leadership leaves teams, organizations, and communities fragmented, disoriented, and disillusioned.

*Leadership Actually* cuts through the fog of illusion to reveal what leadership truly is: a learnable craft that cultivates awareness, fosters agency, and treats the dynamics of teams as living systems, guiding them toward something real and shared. It's an invitation to look beyond the illusion and step into the lived reality of leadership—where responsibility is real, relationships matter, and impact endures.

## HOW THE BOOK IS ORGANIZED

We've designed *Leadership Actually* to guide you through both the theory and practice of genuine leadership. But don't worry, we're practitioners, so we go light on theory and heavy on practical application.

We've divided the book into three sections, each featuring three pairs of chapters. Odd-numbered chapters provide leadership insights through the real-life experiences of our protagonist, Jack Barrett, while even-numbered ones delve into the principles behind these lessons, offering practical advice for applying them.

Part 1, "Setting the Stage to Lead," lays the groundwork by exploring the essential elements of leadership and the importance of mastering them so leadership becomes your craft. Part 2, "Laying the Foundation to Lead," delves into the fundamental skills and practices that, once mastered, will enhance your effectiveness as a leader. Part 3, "Doing the Doing of Leading," integrates insights from parts 1 and 2 and focuses on their application in real-world scenarios, covering often-overlooked core aspects of leadership such as managing team process, teaching and learning together, and co-creating with others.

Each chapter pair ends with an "Extras" section that includes a summary of the two chapters, suggests how you can apply their insights, and provides selected additional resources for deeper study if you're so inclined as well as a related verse from the *Tao Te Ching* (one of the world's oldest leadership texts),[1] and a final word from us.

## MEET JACK BARRETT

Jack Barrett is a former US Army captain, Airborne Ranger, and Vietnam veteran. His early career experiences are the foundation of the leadership lessons presented in the odd-numbered chapters of this book.

*Leadership Actually*, however, is not Jack's biography, nor is it a book about military leadership. Instead, it focuses on strengthening your leadership practice, equipping you with new insights, tools, and approaches to help you make differences that matter. Drawing from our experiences and Jack's stories, it explores the timeless, universal challenges—and triumphs—of leading others wherever you are.

You'll find that Jack's lessons—many of which were forged in the heat of battle—are highly relevant to the leadership challenges you face every day. The foundational knowledge and skills they highlight are applicable across time, place, and context.

As you read, we encourage you to reflect on your own journey: how you got your start leading, where you are at this moment, and, most importantly, where you're headed. The experiences you've had up to now, as well as those you'll have next, are worth exploring thoroughly, thinking about deeply, and recording conscientiously. One day, they're going to make great stories that you'll share with a new generation of leaders.

## ABOUT US

We are the Co-Creative Leadership Alliance, a diverse group of multigenerational leaders and leadership development practitioners from around the world. Our experience covers every level of leadership from first-line managerial roles to the C-suite.

We share a deep belief in the power of being real and telling it like it is. Having learned from some of the foremost experts in our field and witnessed firsthand the transformative impact of effective leadership as it's actually practiced, we hope that *Leadership Actually* becomes a trusted companion on your own leadership journey.

## A FINAL WORD

You are needed. There is no one else like you on the planet. Your leadership matters because how you lead influences not only your own team and organization but also the lives of everyone you touch.

In the midst of today's turbulent world, we can easily lose sight of the connection between genuine leadership and the achievement of some of life's most fundamental goals—well-being, happiness, and success for you and everyone around you.

We like the phrase "Nothing changes if nothing changes." We encourage you to make one small change today—whether you decide to listen to a colleague or child more attentively, express appreciation more often, or engage more deeply with your team. Start small and start now.

Thank you for your interest in *Leadership Actually*. We're honored to be part of your leadership journey and look forward to walking this path with you.

# PART 1

# Setting the Stage to Lead

Part 1, "Setting the Stage to Lead," gets straight to the heart of leadership, which is getting people to work together to pursue and achieve goals. This matters because your life and livelihood, as well as those of the people you lead, depend on it.

You can find tens of thousands of books with the word *leadership* in the title. If you read them all, you'd find they have one thing in common: each, in its own way, aims to inform you about *how to lead.* This book does too.

But what makes *Leadership Actually* different is right there in the title. It's about how to actually do it. Leadership isn't just about using special techniques and strategies but rather cultivating a mindset that illuminates your working relationships in new and more connected ways. You must also refine a core set of leadership skills and knowledge and hone your own unique ways of seeing and interacting with the people and world around you. These add up to what can—and by all means should—be your professional craft, one that's worth committing to and mastering.

Let's dive straight into making that a reality.

# 1 Attention Must Be Paid

All you have to do is pay attention; the lessons always arrive when you are *ready*.

—Paul Coelho

*Tân Sơn Nhât Airbase, Republic of Vietnam. 1971.*

The big jetliner shuddered as it descended through a bank of altocumulus clouds, waking newly promoted US Army Captain Jack Barrett and giving him his first glimpse of Vietnam.

As he surveyed the scene outside the plane's window, Jack thought, "Damn! This is real." Until this moment, the war had been an abstraction for him, shaped by nonstop TV news reports, antiwar music on his car radio, and the protests growing around the world.

Exhausted from the nearly twenty-four-hour flight from California, Jack was now fully awake, his adrenal glands working overtime. At just twenty-three years old and only two years out of university, he was completely unprepared for what lay ahead.

The moment the plane's door opened, a rush of hot, humid, tropical air flooded the cabin, overwhelming the air conditioning. Jack wondered if this was a metaphor for what awaited him. His thoughts were interrupted by a booming voice over the PA system.

"Welcome to the Republic of South Vietnam! There were mortar attacks on the airfield earlier, so we need to get you off the plane and onto the buses outside, pronto. Grab your gear and start making your way to the exit door up front, ASAP."

Soldiers hurriedly exited the plane and boarded military buses waiting at the foot of the airstairs. Jack noticed his bus's windows were open and covered with heavy mesh screens. A nearby soldier quipped, "How big are the flies in this place that you need screens like that?"

The bus driver, overhearing the question, responded in a serious tone, "We're traveling through an unfriendly village to get where we're going. The screens are there to keep bad guys from pitching a hand grenade in and killing our asses."

The mood on the bus turned somber as the new arrivals absorbed the gravity of the situation. The ride to the replacement station at Biên Hòa was uneventful. Tension hung thick in the air. Upon arrival, the soldiers disembarked, completed paperwork, underwent medical checks, and were issued jungle uniforms and combat gear.

During the equipment issue, one jumpy young soldier asked anxiously, "When will we get our M16s?"

"You'll be issued weapons when you reach your units in the field," came the terse reply. "That's where you'll need them."

After the formalities, the soldiers went their separate ways—some to briefings, others to the dining hall, and many straight to their transit barracks to recover from the grueling flight.

Jack attended an orientation briefing for newly arrived officers. He learned about the current political and combat situations, as well as the rules of engagement—army directives outlining the actions soldiers could legally take on their own authority in a warzone.

The most unsettling part of the briefing was the announcement that a few weeks earlier someone had thrown a hand grenade into a nearby transit barracks, killing two American officers outright.

The base hadn't been infiltrated by Vietcong or North Vietnamese commandos; the perpetrator was a dangerously disaffected American soldier. Jack learned that soldiers had quickly coined a new word for such attacks—"fragging." But no matter the euphemism, he understood that fragging was cold-blooded murder, or attempted murder, of army leaders by their own troops using a fragmentation grenade.

Jack was unnerved by the thought of soldiers attacking their own leaders. It confirmed everything he'd suspected about the war. When the briefing concluded, he and a few fellow officers made their way to their sleeping quarters for the night, in the same barracks where the fatal attack had occurred.

Coupled with what he already knew about widespread drug use, racism, and indiscipline throughout Vietnam, the new information about fragging put Jack in a somber, introspective frame of mind.

Jack thought, "This is where I'm going to spend the next year—if I live that long. American soldiers throwing hand grenades at their leaders? This is a nightmare. How the hell am I going to get through it?"

The last thought he had before drifting into a fitful sleep was a cryptic one: "Attention must be paid, Jack. Attention must be paid."

As the war entered its final years, incidents of fragging multiplied. Leaders who were judged by their troops to be too gung-ho, too disciplinarian, or simply unpopular became targets. The situation became so alarming that some leaders, fearing attacks from within their own ranks, changed where they slept every night.

When Jack awoke from his restless sleep, his thoughts were still swirling around that mysterious phrase: "Attention must be paid." During his ruminations, he recalled a conversation he had eighteen months earlier with his commanding officer (CO) in Germany, Lieutenant Paul Lustig.

Paul had told him that their generation of officers was responsible for making positive changes in army leadership. "Otherwise," Paul had said, "I'm afraid we're headed to a very bad place. Remember, Jack, nothing changes if nothing changes."

Despite whatever challenges lay ahead, Jack knew that he'd still be expected to do his job and lead. The question that troubled him was, Exactly how would he do that? His mind raced.

In a moment of clarity, Jack remembered something one of his military science professors at school, an infantry major, had to say about leadership: "Men, when you get to Vietnam, do you want to know why your soldiers will follow you?" After a pregnant pause, and with a smirk on his face, the major delivered his punchline, "Because you have the *f——g* map!"

Jack had laughed with the rest of his class then, but now, alone in his spartan barracks room, seven thousand miles from home, he saw things more clearly. Having the map didn't seem like a sane basis for how to lead anyone anywhere—particularly when people's lives were on the line. From there, he made the short step to the realization that he couldn't rely on what he'd been taught at school.

He'd always known that leading soldiers in Vietnam wouldn't be easy, but he hadn't expected to feel so unprepared. The theories and tactics he'd spent so much time learning felt distant and disconnected from the reality he faced now.

Less than forty-eight hours after his arrival, the chaos around him was already eroding his confidence. And the challenges he anticipated in the field—where he would work with the soldiers whose lives depended on his leadership—only deepened his unease.

With no manual to guide him and no playbook for what lay ahead, Jack turned inward, reflecting on his own sense of right and wrong and the simple lessons he'd learned along his way to that moment: pay attention, care about people, and treat them with respect. As he did, the meaning of "Attention must be paid" became clear to him.

From these principles, Jack began to shape a new way of leading—one that centered on presence, empathy, and trust. He understood that survival wouldn't come from barking orders or enforcing rigid discipline. It would come from working and leading *with* his team and building a bond strong enough to withstand the chaos to come.

Looking back, these changes weren't just the start of Jack's evolution as a leader. They became the foundation of a way of working together that served him—and others—well for the rest of his long career.

## LEADERSHIP TODAY

Recently, the truth of Paul Coelho's epigraph from this chapter—"All you have to do is pay attention; the lessons always arrive when you are *ready*"—came sharply into focus for us once again. It was almost as though it had been waiting for the right moment. This headline caught our attention: "U.S. Employee Engagement Sinks to a 10-Year Low."[1]

The article went on to identify three key factors behind this troubling trend:

- Most employees don't know what's expected of them at work.
- Just over one-third feel someone at work genuinely cares about them as a person.
- Less than one-third believe they are encouraged to grow and develop.

We can't go on like this. Leadership is as much about making connections as it is about giving directions. Chapter 2, "Unpacking Leadership," picks up from Jack's "Attention must be paid" story and looks more closely at what it takes to lead like your life and livelihood depend on it in today's world.

Adopting and adapting this approach might well be the most important leadership step you've taken to date. More are sure to follow.

Chapter 2 explores how you can begin to reverse this trend by unpacking and closely examining what it means to lead. This alternating structure of pairing narratives of leadership lessons learned with analysis and explanation forms the foundation of the book.

As you read on, we invite you to reflect deeply, take stock boldly, and act decisively, keeping two things top of mind: leadership doesn't equate to having the metaphorical map, and nothing changes if nothing changes.

# 2 Unpacking Leadership

Everything's connected
Everything's changing
So pay attention
This is what it's like right now
—Jason Molin

*The Southwestern United States. 2022.*

When Jack looks back on the entirety of his experience, he says his first few days in Vietnam were among the toughest of his career. In that short space of time, he had to accomplish two incredibly consequential tasks:

1. Set aside much of what he'd been taught about leading, crazy ideas such as soldiers following him because he had the map.
2. Replace these assumptions with an approach his heart told him would work but that his head thought was held together with bubble gum and baling wire.

Jack's heart was right. This chapter explores why this was the better option, starting with a side-by-side comparison of an idea that Jack grasped intuitively but couldn't—and wouldn't be able to—articulate for years to come: the idea of illusory versus actual leadership.

## ILLUSORY VERSUS ACTUAL LEADERSHIP

Table 2.1 reflects our own experiences as well as Jack's. Over time, we've seen these patterns emerge again and again in leadership, both good and bad. As you read through this comparison, you might sense echoes of your own experiences in one column and a vision of the kind of leadership you aspire to and hope for in the other.

**TABLE 2.1. ILLUSORY VERSUS ACTUAL LEADERSHIP**

| Illusory leadership | Actual leadership |
|---|---|
| Position authority of based on having the map | Earned and shared authority |
| Individualist approach: I, me, mine | Collective Mindset: We, us, ours |
| Command, control, and compliance-based working relationships | Collaborative, trust-based working relationships |
| Short-term focus, often driven by personal gain | Long-term focus, prioritizing shared goals |
| Top-down, task-oriented goals | Purpose-driven goals co-created with the team |
| Fleeting impact, dependent on hierarchical authority | Sustainable impact through developing people's personal agency |
| "Fake it until you make it" mentality that prioritizes charisma over substance | Authentic, transparent leadership where there's no right way to do a wrong thing |
| Development philosophy: Every person for themselves | Development philosophy: Continuous learning and growth for all |

You might even try filling in your own table. What does illusory leadership look like in your world? How does actual leadership show up for you? At a minimum, filling in your own table can be a fun activity, and you might gain an insight or two along the way.

This comparison reminds us at the Co-Creative Leadership Alliance of an illuminating activity we once did as a team: we each counted the number of effective and ineffective leaders we'd worked under. The results were a sobering three-to-one ratio of ineffective to effective leaders. This realization turned out to be a key motivation for writing this book.

Consider these related questions:

- What do your own numbers look like?
- What do they reveal to you?

Our numbers underscored how the gap between illusory and actual leadership isn't theoretical. It directly impacts how teams function, grow, and ultimately succeed (or fail), raising the $64,000 question: What is leadership?

## DEFINING LEADERSHIP

In their book, *Executive Leadership*, Elliott Jaques and Stephen D. Clement define leadership as "a process you use to get others to move along together with you, and with each other, with competence and full commitment, to achieve a goal."[1]

The authors give a strong definition—the best we've found—but it offers precious little explanation or practical guidance on the how-to. That's where this book comes in. Let's dive in with a look at what we call the three pillars of leadership.

## THE THREE PILLARS OF LEADERSHIP

As Jaques and Clement opine, leadership is a dynamic process. We build on their definition by emphasizing that, because individual leaders actively shape and experience this process, a one-size-fits-all approach doesn't apply. Nevertheless, the process rests on three interdependent mix-and-match pillars:

- Leadership mindset
- Skilled leadership knowledge
- Personal sensibilities of the leader

These pillars, shown in figure 2.1, aren't abstract concepts; they're the essential tools in your leadership toolkit. Like carpenters who use specialized tools to ply their craft, leaders rely on these pillars to build trust, overcome obstacles, and inspire action. Each pillar plays a distinct but interconnected role in how you lead. Let's explore them one by one.

## LEADERSHIP MINDSET

Your mindset is the mental framework that shapes how you approach challenges, interact with others, and view your role. It's not just what you think but it's how you think as well.

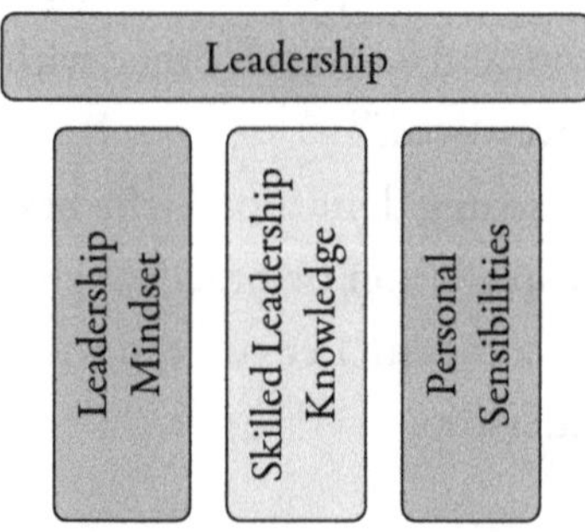


**FIGURE 2.1. THE THREE PILLARS OF LEADERSHIP**

Leaders with a strong mindset see challenges as opportunities, value feedback as a vehicle for growth, and approach problems with solutions in mind. This mindset not only influences how you lead but also sets an example for your team.

Stanford professor Carol Dweck's research into fixed and growth mindsets offers valuable insight.[2] Those with a fixed mindset see situations as static—"It is what it is." In contrast, those with a growth mindset believe in potential and change—"If you can think it, you can do it."

Mindsets often operate under the surface, shaping behavior in ways we may not realize. Exploring your mindset can be both enlightening and transformative. In this spirit, we've provided tools to help you assess and develop your leadership mindset:

- A simple mindset continuum to help you reflect on where you stand
- An informal leadership mindset self-assessment
- A deeper analysis of how mindset influences leadership

## THE MINDSET CONTINUUM

Imagine Professor Dweck's concepts of fixed and growth mindsets mapped onto a continuum, from fixed mindsets on the left to growth mindsets on the right as shown in figure 2.2.

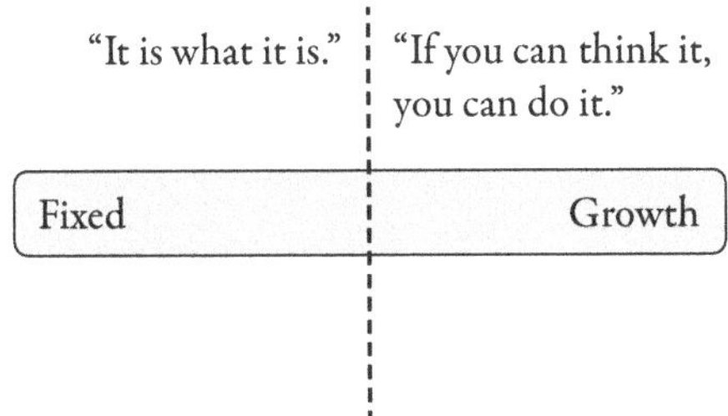


**FIGURE 2.2. THE MINDSET CONTINUUM**

Where would you place your current mindset? How do you think your team members, boss, or closest colleagues would describe your mindset?

While you reflect, let's dive deeper into the differences between fixed and growth mindsets.

## Fixed versus Growth Leadership Mindsets

One of the first ways you can differentiate illusory and actual leadership is through leadership mindset. Leaders with fixed mindsets seek control, avoid challenges, and resist feedback. While they may appear strong, their resistance to change hinders their growth and limits their team's development. These leaders often prioritize short-term results over long-term innovation.

In contrast, growth-minded leaders believe leadership skills can be developed through continuous learning, effort, and perseverance. They embrace failure as an opportunity to improve and encourage their teams to take risks, innovate, and learn from setbacks. Growth-minded leaders focus on fostering autonomy, collaboration, and creative problem-solving, fostering a culture of continuous learning where failure becomes a stepping stone to success.

Leaders with growth mindsets also have the ability to shift focus from individual accomplishments to collective achievement. A historic example of this perspective is found in President John F. Kennedy's 1961 inaugural address: "Ask not what your country can do for you—ask what you can do for your country. My fellow citizens of the world: ask not what America will do for you, but what together we can do for the freedom of man."[3]

President Kennedy's call to action encapsulated a growth mindset by prioritizing collective effort and long-term vision over personal gain. Similarly, as a leader, you can foster a mindset of collaboration and shared purpose within your team.

Reflect on your leadership approach: Are you fostering growth and collaboration, or are you focused on maintaining control and avoiding challenges? More importantly, what actions can you take today to strengthen or shift your mindset?

## LEADERSHIP MINDSET SELF-ASSESSMENT

To explore your mindset further, take a moment to answer this quick, informal self-assessment:

1. How actively do you pay attention to team dynamics and interactions?
   - ☐ I pay attention when I need to.
   - ☐ I usually notice things.
   - ☐ I actively pay attention to these things.
2. How persistent are you with difficult problems requiring creativity?
   - ☐ I tend to give up too easily.
   - ☐ I'm able to stay with problems for a while.
   - ☐ I'm tenacious. I'm extremely persistent.
3. How open are you to feedback from your team or colleagues?
   - ☐ I'd rather not entertain feedback; it feels like criticism.
   - ☐ I'm willing to hear people out most of the time.
   - ☐ I encourage people to offer me feedback.
4. How often do you promote collaboration or working together?
   - ☐ I think people should compete. That's how you get the best work.
   - ☐ I suggest collaboration when the circumstances require it.
   - ☐ Everyone should collaborate all the time.

5. How committed are you to learning and teaching others?
   - ☐ I know all I want to, and others can make up their own minds.
   - ☐ I'm willing to learn and help others when it will do some good.
   - ☐ I'm all in on learning and teaching.
6. How willing are you to experiment with new leadership behaviors?
   - ☐ I'm not big on experiments.
   - ☐ Sometimes, I can be convinced to try new things.
   - ☐ I love trying out new things. I'm very willing.
7. How important are high standards and improving them to you?
   - ☐ I keep my standards high. They don't need to be improved.
   - ☐ I'll play the continuous improvement game when I need to.
   - ☐ My thinking is if you're not improving, you're falling behind.

After answering, step back and reflect on what the blend of your responses represents. Consider writing a short, descriptive paragraph entitled "My Leadership Mindset" to summarize your insights. What patterns emerge? How do they align with your leadership goals?

## Five Behavioral Patterns of a Growth Mindset

Leadership mindsets often work behind the scenes, quietly shaping how you think and act. Understanding and assessing your mindset can help you harness its potential.

In our work with leaders, we've identified five key behavioral patterns associated with a growth leadership mindset shown in figure 2.3, attentiveness, commitment, communication, cooperation and collaboration, and craftsmanship.

## Attentiveness

Attentiveness, or paying attention, means paying particular notice, taking heed, or concentrating on something.[4] This behavior was the subject of the enigmatic and cautionary "attention must be paid" message that invaded Jack's thoughts as he struggled to fall asleep his first night in Vietnam.

Jon Kabat-Zinn, professor emeritus of medicine at the University of Massachusetts Medical School, calls paying attention "mindfulness" and says, "It's awareness that arises through paying attention, in the present moment."[5]

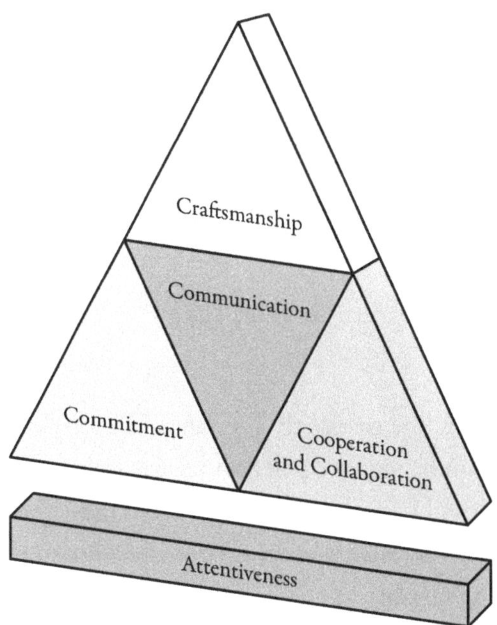


**FIGURE 2.3. GROWTH LEADERSHIP MINDSET**

Imagine Jack, just twenty-three years old, arriving in a warzone, realizing that his survival depended on his ability to notice the smallest details. An unusual sound, a fleeting expression on a teammate's face, a tree or bush that looked out of place—any of these details could be the difference between life and death. Attentiveness became not just a practice but a lifeline.

## Commitment

Commitment is feeling internally compelled to act in a particular way.[6] After his restless first night in Vietnam, Jack reached three conclusions—surviving the war required his full concentration, his ideas about leadership needed an immediate overhaul, and he needed to quickly come up with a new approach to doing things.

This was Jack's moment of decision, when he accepted that the well-being of the people he would lead was his responsibility. Their lives would be in his hands, and his would be in theirs. It was the moment he committed to becoming a leader.

Think of a moment in your life when everything changed—when a decision you made altered the course of your life or the lives of others. Commitment in leadership is like that. You come to the point of no return, where you decide that the stakes are too high to give your work anything less than your best.

## Communication

Communication is the distinctly human and interpersonal process of using words, sounds, signs, or behaviors to exchange information or express ideas, thoughts, and feelings to others.[7] In the best of cases, communicating effectively is a crapshoot. That's because so many dependent and independent variables are in play:

- *Meaning*—Do the words you're trying to communicate carry the same meaning for those who receive them?
- *Social and cultural differences*—How do differences like gender, ethnicity, and cultural background affect your communication?
- *Values*—How do different values or value systems alter the situation?
- *Languages*—Is there any miscommunication over language differences?
- *Your surroundings*—Are you in a relatively quiet office, on a factory floor beside loud machinery, or in a moving vehicle?

You get the point. It's amazing any of us are able to form meaningful connections with others. But however difficult communicating on this level is, we have to keep trying. Genuine care for others, combined with decisive value-adding leadership, answers most of the questions a leader will face. Communicating effectively is the first step toward putting both into action.

## Cooperation and Collaboration

Many people think that cooperation and collaboration are the same. They're not. Cooperation is working together toward a common goal while you maintain a certain level of independence. Collaboration requires a deeper, more interactive, and connected way of working together.

Reflect on a time when you were part of a truly collaborative effort—when everyone was in sync, and the sum turned out to be greater than the individual parts. For you as a leader, this translates to creating the conditions in which your team's collective effort outshines any one person's contributions.

### Craftsmanship

The fifth behavioral pattern associated with an effective leadership mindset is craftsmanship. The days when craft was confined to skilled manual work, creating tangible objects or products, are over. The combination of craft and leadership is becoming widely relevant and accepted.

The primary reason is self-evident—craft consistently crushes clumsiness in everything, particularly in leadership because it affects people's lives. When it comes to your bosses, you'd prefer them to be masterful rather than merely going through the motions. The people who work around you feel the same way.

Craftsmanship in leadership is about more than just doing a job well; it's about adopting a leadership mindset that's focused on mastering the art of leading.

If leadership is to be treated as a craft, it follows that leaders should pursue it with the same level of intentional development found in other skilled professions. Here are some ways you can take action.

## Ways to Level Up Your Leadership

The time has come for leaders like you to take a lesson from fields such as medicine, engineering, teaching, and others to figure out how you can inject more standards-based professionalism into your work. Doing so might involve one of these:

- Designing and developing organizationally based leadership apprenticeship programs
- Creating nationally or internationally organized leadership certification programs akin to Project Management Professional (PMP) certifications for project managers[8]
- Undertaking a wide-ranging, crowd-sourced project to establish standards for leadership craftspeople

- Establishing leadership residencies in partnership with universities
- Offering leadership craft masterclasses, workshops, and creating communities of practice

If any of these ideas send a pulse of energy through you, please reach out to us at www.ccla-co.com. We have so much to talk about. Who knows? We might end up changing the world!

In the meantime, having completed our review of what mindsets are, let's forge ahead and complete the last two parts of our overview of leadership mindset: why it matters and how you can enhance it.

## Why Your Leadership Mindset Matters

Your mindset is the foundation of your leadership behavior. Without a strong, clear mindset, even the most skilled leader may struggle to inspire trust, foster collaboration, or guide a team through challenges.

A healthy, well-communicated leadership mindset instills confidence in your team. When your team members see you focused on the bigger picture, resilient in adversity and committed to their development, it fosters trust and collective effort. However, leadership mindsets don't develop by chance. They must be intentionally cultivated and practiced over time.

## Tips to Help You Enhance Your Leadership Mindset

An effective leadership mindset grows through reflection, learning, and intentional practice. Here are a few practical strategies to help you enhance yours:

- *Develop self-awareness*—Regularly reflect on your thoughts, behaviors, and reactions. Ask yourself, "Am I focusing on solutions or dwelling on problems?" and "Are my decisions driven by ego or the good of the team?"

- *Seek feedback*—Actively ask for input from your team and peers. Leaders with growth mindsets view feedback as fuel for improvement—not criticism.
- *Embrace challenges*—Reframe challenges as opportunities for growth instead of threats. Pushing yourself beyond your comfort zone builds resilience and adaptability.
- *Lead with optimism*—Root your leadership in optimism—not blind positivity, but the belief that progress is always possible. Practice reframing setbacks as chances to learn and grow.

Your leadership mindset requires ongoing attention, reflection, and renewal. Unlike a car, you don't come equipped with an automatic system to alert you when you need a tune-up. Staying connected to your mindset is up to you, but the effort pays dividends.

With that in mind, let's move on to the second pillar: your skilled leadership knowledge.

## SKILLED LEADERSHIP KNOWLEDGE

You may not recognize the term *skilled knowledge*, but you encounter the concept daily. Skilled knowledge is the kind of know-how you use automatically—like tying your shoelaces, riding a bike, or driving a car.

Skilled leadership knowledge works the same way. It's the practical application of leadership know-how: making quick decisions under pressure, managing productive meetings, resolving conflicts, and delegating effectively. Think of it as leadership muscle memory. With practice, leading becomes instinctive.

Skilled leadership knowledge also includes distinct competencies, strengths, and behaviors aligned with your leadership model. Whatever model you follow, it should clearly define the skills required to master it. Without this clarity, proficiency is impossible.

You develop skilled leadership knowledge through experience, training, feedback, and consistent practice. Over time, you'll build a repertoire of leadership skills you can deploy effortlessly. Like a musician who practices even after mastering an instrument, leaders must continuously refine their abilities and expand their toolkit.

This book will guide you through ways to sharpen these skills and grow as a leader.

## Why Skilled Leadership Knowledge Matters

A strong mindset sets the stage, but skilled leadership knowledge ensures you can act decisively, navigate complexity, and bring your vision to life.

Leaders without practical skills often feel stuck in a cycle of reacting to chaos, constantly putting out fires instead of proactively guiding their teams. This reactive approach creates a focus on short-term fixes over long-term success—a hallmark of illusory leadership.

Conversely, leaders with well-honed skills can pivot in real time during crises, provide clear direction to their teams, and maintain momentum. They don't just react, they anticipate, plan, and execute with precision, ensuring their teams thrive in both calm and turbulent times.

## Tips to Help You Enhance Your Skilled Leadership Knowledge

Building skilled leadership knowledge is a gradual but essential process. These strategies can help you grow and refine your abilities:

- *Commit to continuous learning*—Leadership is ever evolving. Stay curious, read widely, and make learning a habit. Attend workshops, seek advice from experienced leaders, and stay proactive in expanding your knowledge. The more you learn, the more adaptable and resourceful you become.

- *Sharpen core skills*—Identify key leadership tasks, such as setting goals, managing challenges, or improving self-awareness—and practice them deliberately. A skilled leadership coach can also provide valuable insights, helping you analyze difficult situations and develop alternative strategies.
- *Ask for and reflect on feedback*—Proactively seek feedback from your team, peers, and mentors. Ask specific questions, such as "What could I have done better?" and "How can I support you more effectively?"
- *Regularly explore what worked and what didn't*—Some leaders hold weekly meetings to discuss lessons learned and adjust plans accordingly. This practice, inspired by leadership expert Marshall Goldsmith's "feedforward" approach, uses insights about current operations to improve future performance.[9]
- *Prepare for the unexpected*—Good leaders anticipate surprises. Practice scenario planning by visualizing potential challenges and discussing what-if strategies with your team. Whether navigating crises or handling last-minute changes, leaders who rehearse alternative scenarios build confidence and readiness.
- *Streamline everyday tasks*—From running productive meetings to delegating efficiently, effective leaders turn routine activities into streamlined processes. Those who master these basics free up time and energy for higher-level strategy and problem-solving.

With these tips, you can continually improve your leadership expertise, ensuring you're ready to meet any challenge. Next, we'll explore the third and often-overlooked, but exceedingly important, pillar of leadership: your personal sensibilities.

## PERSONAL SENSIBILITIES

As we noted in the preface, you are needed. There is no one else like you on the planet. Your leadership matters because how you lead influences not only your team and organization but also the lives of everyone you touch.

What makes this true? What sets your leadership apart? While many can develop a leadership mindset and skilled leadership knowledge, only you can lead the way you do. Your personal sensibilities—your unique combination of insight, intuition, and discernment—make your leadership distinctive.

Your personal sensibilities shape how you perceive and respond to situations, people, emotions—almost everything in your life. They do so by reflecting your preferences, values, and worldview, influencing how you experience art, music, literature, and even ethical dilemmas. Your sensibilities combine to create what's unique about you and how you lead.

Leadership works best when you embrace your individuality instead of trying to imitate others. Jack learned this lesson the hard way early in his army career when he tried in vain to copy the spit-and-polish style of a more senior officer when he gave presentations.

The first time Jack got an opportunity to give a briefing to his commanding general, he was so stiff and nervous, the general excused himself from the meeting. Jack had failed miserably, coming across like an automaton versus a real person with valuable information to impart. Once he decided to just be himself when he presented, meetings went much better, and he learned an important lesson.

### Qualities of Personal Sensibilities

When you're yourself, your natural human levels of emotional intelligence, cultural awareness, and compassion shine trough. Let's explore how these qualities enhance your leadership and how you can develop them further.

### Emotional Intelligence

Emotional intelligence is your ability to recognize, understand, and manage emotions—both your own and those of others. Leaders with high emotional intelligence excel in navigating interpersonal dynamics with empathy and composure. They diffuse tension, build trust, and inspire loyalty.

Ask yourself, "How well do I read my own emotions, as well as those of my team? Do I show empathy, or do I default to logic at the expense of connection?"

### Cultural Awareness

Cultural awareness involves recognizing and respecting differences in how individuals and groups communicate and make decisions. Every organization and team has its own culture, and understanding these nuances makes you a more effective leader.

Leaders with cultural awareness can read the room and adjust their approach to meet the unspoken needs of their team. They are attuned to team dynamics, fostering collaboration and inclusion.

### Empathy and Compassion

While empathy and compassion are closely related, they are distinct. Empathy is understanding and sharing someone else's feelings, stepping into their shoes to see the world from their perspective. Compassion, on the other hand, goes a step further by adding the desire to help.

Demonstrating both qualities helps you connect with your team on a deeper level. When team members feel understood and supported, they perform not out of obligation but from a sense of trust and loyalty.

## Why Personal Sensibilities Matter

Leadership is fundamentally about people—their emotions, needs, and motivations. Recognizing, understanding, and using your personal sensibilities sets you apart as an authentic leader who fosters genuine connections, as opposed to an illusory leader who is focused solely on managing tasks.

Leaders attuned to who they are create team environments that prioritize psychological safety—a space where people feel confident expressing ideas, concerns, and opinions without fear. In such environments, innovation, collaboration, and commitment thrive. Who you are is what your team will reflect back to you.

## Tips to Enhance Your Personal Sensibilities

Like your mindset and leadership skills, your personal sensibilities can be intentionally developed. Here are actionable strategies to cultivate them:

- *Work on your self-awareness*—Ask yourself questions such as "How did I react?" "Why did I react that way?" "How did my reactions affect my behavior?" Understanding your emotional patterns helps you manage them and empathize with others more effectively.
- *Practice active listening*—Truly focus on what someone is saying instead of planning your response. Reflect back or paraphrase what they've said to confirm your understanding. This builds trust and ensures decisions are based on clear communication. Refer to the "Listening Ladder" tool in appendix A for more practical listening techniques.

- *Cultivate empathy*—Put yourself in your team's shoes. Ask yourself, "What challenges are they facing? And how might they feel about their work and the team?" If you're unsure, ask them directly in one-to-one conversations. When you understand others' perspectives, it fosters rapport and builds trust.
- *Build trust through transparency*—Being open and honest about your intentions, decisions, and goals also builds trust. You will see the effect of operating transparently in chapter 3 when Jack meets his team for the first time.
- *Foster respect*—Respect begins with clear communication. Share the big picture. Talk about why the team is doing a certain task, what roles you expect them to play, and what kind of support they can expect from you throughout.

  Follow through with small, consistent acts of respect, such as any of the following:
  - Greeting people by name each day
  - Saying "please" and "thank you"
  - Acknowledging people's perspectives
  - Being on time for team meetings and taking responsibility for mistakes
  - Giving credit where it's due
  - Talking to people directly instead of about them

These small actions build trust, confidence, and a willingness in your team to leave it all on the field when necessary.

Cultivating your personal sensibilities helps you lead authentically, build meaningful connections, and foster an environment of trust, collaboration, and humanity.

This completes our exploration of the three pillars of leadership, the foundation of what it takes to actually lead and be effective doing so—namely, your leadership mindset, the indispensable core of your skilled leadership knowledge, and your unique personal sensibilities.

When combined, these three pillars help you and your team move beyond common myths of illusory leadership, which include the belief that leaders are born and not developed, that they instinctively know what's best and that they always have the answers, and that they alone can empower their teams.

Grasping the three pillars is just the beginning. As you and your team come to understand them more deeply and use them more intentionally, they will take on even greater meaning and value. With this in mind, let's take a look at the three pillars from the perspective of a dynamic model that integrates them—the Leadership Actually Model.

## THE LEADERSHIP ACTUALLY MODEL

Much like an x-ray reveals hidden structures, the Leadership Actually Model uncovers the interdependent relationships between the three pillars. It exposes the essential elements of leadership knowledge and skill unique to truly leading, including understanding content and process, becoming more self-aware, turning information into communication, managing team process, teaching and learning together, and co-creating with others.

As we progress through the book together, we'll shed new light on each of these elements from a perspective that's not only fresh but will also encourage you to reconsider what and how you think about leading. We'll also offer you practical strategies you can implement immediately to create a real and lasting impact for you and your team.

Figure 2.4 depicts a visual representation of the Leadership Actually Model, which is not a static framework but rather a tool designed to challenge your assumptions and invite you to see leadership as a dynamic, evolving interplay of skills, mindsets, and sensibilities.

As you study this graphic, notice how the three pillars are represented—leadership mindset anchors the entire model from its center, which is surrounded by the six interdependent elements of skilled

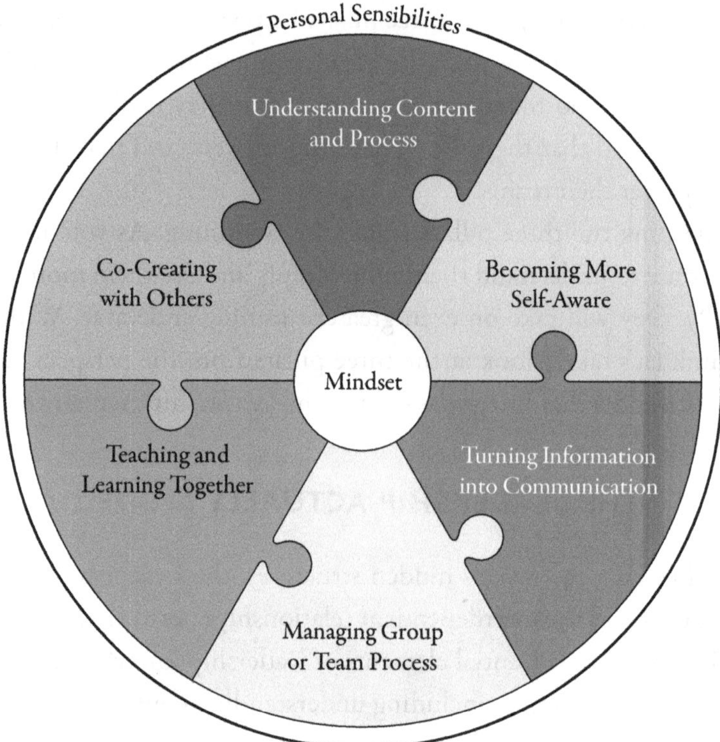


**FIGURE 2.4. THE LEADERSHIP ACTUALLY MODEL**

leadership knowledge. Personal sensibilities encircle the entire framework, where, much like how yeast transforms dough in the baking process, they subtly inform and influence everything you do.

This dynamic interplay between the parts of the model offers a fresh perspective on leadership today, and also foreshadows a tantalizing possibility for how it might evolve tomorrow. Here's how this can play out.

As a leader today, you're no stranger to navigating contradictions. How do you foster innovation without losing stability, or inspire individuality while maintaining shared purpose? These tensions aren't just challenges, they're part and parcel to your work. The Leadership Actually Model invites you to explore these and other paradoxes that have always characterized the nature of leading others and always will.

## WHAT IF?

Bringing a future full of possibilities into focus will require a renaissance of intentionality on our parts to come together as leaders to redefine the professional purpose of our work.

What would we learn if we paused long enough to consider what we do every day, the numbers of people we interact with, and the influence we exert on their lives, for good or for bad? Would we see the unlimited potential—perhaps beyond that of any other line of work?

What would happen if we were to reimagine this profession of ours as being more than the roles we occupy or the set of tools we use?

What if we visualized our work as a professional craft, one that we dedicate ourselves to hone over years of practice, learning through experience and refinement and teaching others? Chapters 5 and 6 will explore this idea of leadership as a craft, helping you frame your own leadership journey as an ongoing practice—one where mastery is achieved through not perfection but commitment to continuous learning, adapting, and improving.

The journey to becoming a truly skilled leader is not a straight path; it's a process of discovery and growth. If you're bold enough to travel it, the road ahead can challenge and inspire you and the rest of us. Let's take this next step together.

## EXTRAS: CHAPTERS 1 AND 2

### Chapters 1 and 2 Summary

- The original idea for *Leadership Actually* came from the true story of a young army officer's arrival in Vietnam in 1971 and how he and his team learned how to work together under the most challenging of circumstances.
- Effective leaders pay attention to the individuals around them, their teams collectively, and the circumstances in which they all work.

- Jack Barrett and his team survived a war by learning to pay attention and work together like their lives depended on it.
- Leadership is often described at the top line as either good or bad, effective or ineffective. This book slices it another way—as either illusory or actual—and offers a side-by-side comparison of the two.
- It also asks and answers the question What is leadership? We use the best and simplest definition of leadership we know: "Leadership is a process you use to get others to move along together with you, and with each other, with competence and full commitment, to achieve a goal,"[10] which is true regardless of any approach you use.
- Leadership of any stripe comprises three essential pillars: a leadership mindset, skilled leadership knowledge, and the personal sensibilities of the leader.
    - Leadership mindset includes five behavioral patterns: attentiveness, commitment, communication, cooperation and collaboration, and craftsmanship.
    - Skilled leadership knowledge contained within the Leadership Actually Model includes understanding content and process, becoming more self-aware, turning information into communication, managing team process, teaching and learning together, and co-creating with others.
    - Personal sensibilities are a leader's unique awareness of and responsiveness toward situations and people, particularly their emotions.
- You don't need an advanced degree, special certification, or psychoanalysis to be an effective leader. Your basic humanity meets all the prerequisites.
- The Leadership Actually Model is like an x-ray:
    - It reveals structures invisible to the naked eye. It uncovers the interdependent relationships between the three pillars.

- o It exposes the essential elements of leadership knowledge and skill unique to truly leading.
- o It can foreshadow how leadership might evolve if we leaders embrace it as a professional craft of influence.[11]

## How to Use the Information in Chapters 1 and 2

The quote "Great things are not done by impulse, but by a series of small things brought together" from Vincent van Gogh highlights the significance of the small parts of leadership covered in the first two chapter pairs. Your leadership mindset is the most significant of these small parts, so it's worth spending some time on. Here are a few ideas of steps you can take to strengthen it:

- Revisit the Leadership Mindset Self-Assessment in this chapter, and compose a paragraph describing your leadership mindset. How many of the five behavioral patterns of a growth-oriented leadership mindset (attentiveness, commitment, communication, cooperation and collaboration, and craftsmanship) does yours reflect?
- Ask yourself, "What changes in my mindset would I like to make? What's preventing me from doing it? And what would it look like if I actively pursued these improvements?"
- Being bolder still, consider asking your team about their perceptions of your mindset and which behaviors they'd like to see more and less of from you. Below is an example of a Team Member Assessment about your leadership mindset that you can adapt and use.
- Compare what others perceive about your mindset with your own thoughts. How wide is the gap between them? If there's a substantial difference, what, if anything, do you want to do to begin aligning the two? What's your plan? Where will you start?

## TEAM MEMBER ASSESSMENT OF [LEADER'S NAME] LEADERSHIP MINDSET

Fill in the blanks with the name of the person whose leadership mindset you're assessing and mark your responses to each question.

1. How much does ________ pay attention to what's going on around him/her, particularly with other people?
   ☐ Not at all ☐ A little ☐ A lot

2. How often is ________ willing to stay with a tough problem and find a solution?
   ☐ Rarely ☐ Sometimes ☐ Most of the time

3. How open is ________ to being influenced by you and your colleagues?
   ☐ Not at all ☐ A little ☐ A lot

4. How actively does ________ emphasize team collaboration and working together?
   ☐ Not at all ☐ Somewhat ☐ Very actively

5. How interested is ________ in both learning and sharing knowledge to help others grow?
   ☐ Not at all ☐ Somewhat committed ☐ Very interested

6. How committed is ________ to trying out or practicing new behaviors?
   ☐ Not at all ☐ Somewhat ☐ Very committed

7. How important are continuous improvement and high standards to ________?
   □ Not important □ Somewhat important □ Very important

Verse 17, *Tao Te Ching*

When great people rule,
subjects know little of their existence.
Rulers who are less great win
the affection and praise
of their subjects.
A common ruler is feared
by his subjects, and an unworthy ruler
is despised.
When a ruler lacks faith,
you may seek in vain for it
among his subjects.
How carefully a wise ruler chooses his words.
He performs deeds, and accumulates merit!
Under such a ruler
the people think they are ruling themselves.

## Final Thoughts

### *Vietnam. 1971 and 1972.*

In the chaos of Vietnam in 1971 and 1972, Jack Barrett experienced a profound shift in his understanding of leadership. Grappling with the cryptic phrase "attention must be paid," he started to grasp the importance of observing the subtleties of human behavior—a lesson that echoed something his mother was fond of saying: "There's always more going on than meets the eye, Jack."

This realization, coupled with his growing awareness of the limits of what he could control, opened new doors for his approach to leading. He became aware that his role wasn't just about managing tasks; it was about paying attention to people—their emotions, motivations, and interactions—and managing those as well. Years later, Professor Robert E. Quinn would describe this awareness as "entering the fundamental state of leadership."[12]

In chapter 3, you'll see Jack putting these lessons into practice as he meets his new team. He begins to navigate the challenges ahead, laying the groundwork for cooperation, which will eventually evolve into full collaboration as the team learns to work together under pressure—and under fire.

# 3 Cooperate and Graduate

The Principal of Priority states (a) you must know the difference between what is urgent and what is important, and (b) you must do the important first.

—Steven Pressfield

*Tân Sơn Nhất Airbase. 1971, three days later.*

Jack's epiphany—leading like his life depended on it—was born during his first restless days in Vietnam. It set the tone for meeting his new team, and, reinforced by his experience working with them, it became his guiding principle.

After two days of waiting at Biên Hòa to learn about his assignment, Jack finally received orders to report directly to the Military Assistance Command, Vietnam (MACV) headquarters at Tân Sơn Nhất Airbase by 0600 the next morning.[1] His assignment was to a unit bearing the innocuous name Combined Plans and Actions Group, which only deepened his curiosity about what lay ahead.

When the sun rose, Jack was in an open-air jeep trundling through the oppressive heat and humidity of Southeast Asia. By the time he reached his destination at MACV, he felt like he was in a steam bath. Sweat poured down his body, plastering his newly issued jungle uniform to him like a second sticky layer of skin. He reminded himself that he'd best get used to the discomfort—quickly. It was unlikely to get any better.

Exiting the jeep, Jack approached the building where he was to report. After showing his identification and written orders to the armed military police at the security checkpoint, he was allowed to pass into the air-conditioned lobby. The sudden change in temperature from the stifling heat outside to the almost frigid interior caused him to shiver.

The lobby was polished and professional. American and South Vietnamese flags decorated the space, alongside comfortable seating and a scattering of green tropical plants. Aside from the foreign flags, it could have been the lobby of almost any major corporation back home. It was anything but.

As he approached the reception desk, Jack mused, "So this is how the rear echelon lives." His thoughts were interrupted by a crisp, matter-of-fact greeting from a starched, spit-and-polished young sergeant behind the counter: "Good morning, sir. How may I help you?"

The whole scene was a striking contrast to the images of triple-canopy jungles and ragged, rain-soaked soldiers Jack had seen on news reports back in "the World."[2]

Presenting his identification and orders once again, Jack watched as the sergeant carefully examined them, then crosschecked the details against what seemed to be a list of appointments. When the young soldier looked up again and spoke, his tone softened: "Ah, Captain Barrett, sir. You're expected. One moment and I'll show you to your meeting room."

The sergeant rose from his seat and motioned for Jack to follow him down one of the corridors leading from the lobby. He led Jack into a well-appointed conference room where a half-dozen soldiers were already seated around a long table. As Jack entered, the soldiers rose to their feet—a military courtesy to the senior officer in the room. Slightly embarrassed, Jack quickly acknowledged the gesture and signaled for them to sit.

Moments later, everyone—including Jack—stood again as two colonels, one army and one air force, entered the room, followed by a small group of staff officers.

"Be seated," the army colonel ordered. "I'm Colonel Graves, commanding officer of the Combined Plans and Actions Group." He gestured to the officer beside him. "This is Colonel Jones, senior air force liaison officer from the Seventy-Second Bombardment Wing on Guam."

The soldiers exchanged curious glances, wondering what the air force officer's presence implied.

Colonel Graves's manner and tone were direct as he continued. "I'm going to be straightforward. The urgency of the moment requires it. The success of your mission—and those of a few other carefully selected teams like you—will be instrumental in determining whether the US achieves what President Nixon has called 'peace with honor' in Vietnam."[3]

Seeing puzzled expressions, Graves smiled wryly. "I'm sure you have questions. Answering them is why you'll be with us for the next few days." The tension in the room eased, and he pressed on.

"You're not here by chance. Each of you was chosen because of your backgrounds for a crucial, semiclandestine role in the president's 'Vietnamization' strategy. This strategy shifts the burden of combat from US forces to the South Vietnamese Army, strengthening their ability to defend their own country while we continue providing training, advice, and, most critically, air support."[4]

Graves paused, letting his words sink in. "Recent top-secret intelligence reports indicate that the North Vietnamese are planning a major offensive within the next six to nine months. Their primary objective will likely be the capture of Saigon, which would end the war outright." A big screen at the front of the room flickered, revealing a large-scale map, shown in figure 3.1.

"This is Tây Ninh Province," Graves said as he stood and walked to the end of the conference table. Using a collapsible pointer, he directed

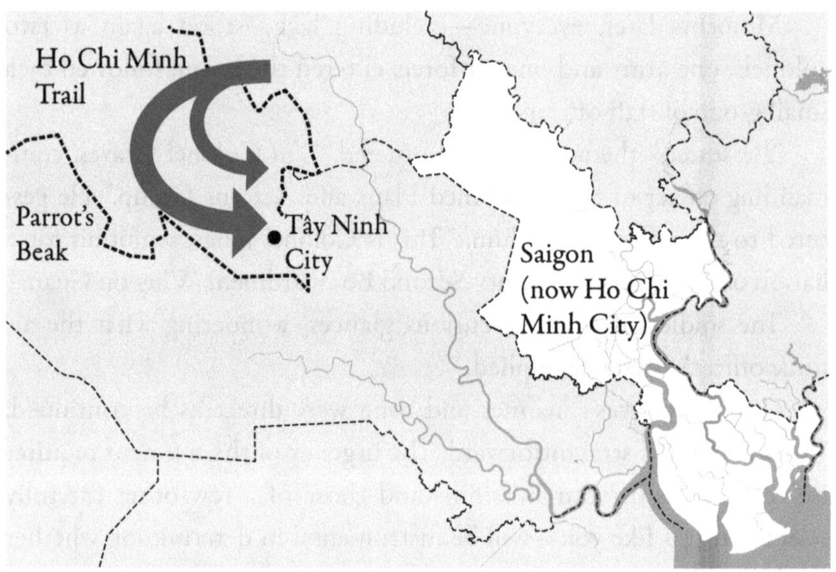


**FIGURE 3.1. TÂY NINH PROVINCE AND THE PARROT'S BEAK**

everyone's attention to the screen. "Tây Ninh City is about a hundred kilometers northwest of Saigon, and the area outlined by the heavy dotted line is the border between Cambodia and South Vietnam is known as the 'Parrot's Beak' because of its distinctive shape.

"As I've said, the enemy's top priority in the coming offensive will be capturing Saigon. The key to thwarting his plans will involve interdicting and disrupting the massing of North Vietnamese troops and the movement of their heavy equipment—tanks, artillery, and other vehicles—at the terminus of the Ho Chi Minh Trail in the Parrot's Beak. This job is best suited to Colonel Jones's B-52 bombers."

Colonel Jones rose as Graves finished, taking over the briefing.

"Good morning, gentlemen," Colonel Jones began. "Colonel Graves is right. The Seventy-Second Bombardment Wing specializes in bombing missions flown out of Andersen Air Force Base on Guam.

"You may—or may not—know that B-52s have been flying missions from Guam to South Vietnam since 1965 as part of Operation

Arc Light. Arc Light has transformed the B-52 from a nuclear delivery platform to a close air support powerhouse, providing vital air support to ground troops throughout the war."

Jones glanced around the room, gauging the soldiers' reactions. "B-52s can fly from Guam to the Parrot's Beak, conduct bombing runs, and return to base in about twelve hours. These missions are complex and expensive, and as the war draws down and budgets tighten, every bomb we drop must count. That's why timely and accurate human intelligence is critical."

The soldiers around the table leaned in, paying closer attention. Jones nodded to Colonel Graves, signaling the end of his remarks. Graves resumed his place at the front of the room, his tone even more serious.

"Thank you, Colonel Jones. It's time to get down to brass tacks. You might be wondering what relevance B-52s have to you. It's this: your mission for the next six months is to be the eyes and ears of Arc Light in Tây Ninh Province and the Parrot's Beak. Specifically, it will be to do three things: conduct close, eyes-on intelligence gathering of enemy activities; prepare detailed analyses of enemy strength, movements, and equipment; and make targeting recommendations for B-52 strikes, which you will relay directly to Colonel Jones's team here at MACV. I know you have lots of questions, every one of which we'll address during the next few days. In the meantime, are there any immediate ones I can answer?"

The room was silent, the soldiers too stunned to speak. After two days of wrestling with anxiety and doubt in the transient barracks, however, Jack had resolved that whatever assignment he was given, he'd do it to the very best of his ability. He knew what his mission entailed, and he'd also met the team he'd be leading, men he was responsible for bringing back home safely. To do so, he'd lead openly and transparently, not just as Captain Jack Barrett, the army officer, but as Jack Barrett, the person. This approach felt right and made sense to him and would become the core of a leadership philosophy he'd continue to build on for the rest of his life.

That evening, the team had its first chance to meet alone. They shared a meal and drank more than a few beers as they reflected on the day's revelations. Amid shared stories and laughter, the conversation gradually shifted to the seriousness of their mission.

Jack set the tone early, speaking with straightforwardness and respect. Today, his approach might be labeled as "modeling the behavior you want from others." In Jack's day, it was just good leadership.

Jack began: "I'm going to borrow something Colonel Graves said earlier about the 'urgency of the moment' and the need to be direct and candid.

"We're about to find ourselves close enough to the North Vietnamese to smell the nuoc mam on their breath while we're reconnoitering their movements. We'll be reporting what we learn to MACV to help them plan B-52 strikes and then getting the hell out of the area so we don't get bombed ourselves."

Heads around the table nodded in understanding as Jack continued.

"The best way for us to get through what we're going into is to work together—really work together—rather than just going through the motions. Also, by not trying to out-soldier each other. The only competition that we have from here on in is the enemy.

"I want us to use this time we have tonight to talk about what working together as a team means to each of us. I'd also like each of us to talk about ourselves so we can start to get to know each other. I'll go first. Jump in to ask questions or make comments whenever you want.

"You can tell by looking at me that I'm not an old hand at soldiering. I've been in the army just over two years. I've been through basic officer training, Airborne and Ranger Schools, and I was in Germany for eighteen months before arriving here less than a week ago.

"On the personal side, I have a wife and three-month-old son back at home. I grew up in a military family—my dad's still on active duty.

And last but not least, I wouldn't be being straight up with you if I didn't admit that the prospect of what we're about to do scares the shit out of me."

The men around the table didn't know what to make of Jack—particularly his admission of being afraid. To relieve some of the pressure, one of the men blurted out, "No shit, sir! Your father's still in the service? Is he a general or something?"

Jack snorted a laugh.

"Not by a long shot. He's an NCO—a master sergeant and WWII vet. And he'd be pissed if he knew you thought he might be an officer. I can't tell you how many times I've heard 'Don't call me sir! I'm an NCO. I work for a living.'"

Laughter rippled through the group, followed by a chorus of comments:

"There it is."

"Dig it."

"How cool is that?"

Jack smiled, glad to finally be with soldiers—salt-of-the-earth guys who said what they thought without any hearts and flowers. One phrase in particular caught his attention. He had heard it at least a dozen times during the three days he'd been in-country: "There it is."

He'd learn over time that "There it is" was the signature expression of soldiers in Vietnam and was used liberally to acknowledge another's reality, express understanding, or simply let off some steam. Toward the end of the war, the phrase also came to embody the stoic and downbeat attitude soldiers adopted to cope with the challenges they faced, as well as the absurdities of the war itself.

Picking up where he left off, Jack got even more personal. "As long as we're talking about my father, and in the spirit of getting to know each other, I'll tell you a quick story. When my dad heard about my orders to Vietnam, he called me in Germany and offered to take my place here. He said he'd checked the regulations and found out that if one family member was stationed in a combat zone, other members of the same family weren't required to accept orders to the same country."

"Then why the hell are you here, sir?" a few of the men asked kiddingly.

Jack answered in all seriousness, "Think about it. If your father fought overseas in WWII, was still in the service, and volunteered to take your place in this shithole, would you have let him? I don't think so."

One of the more junior soldiers offered: "Yeah, I mean, yes, sir—you're probably right, but having someone take your place here is a nice thought."

Jack smiled. "It is. I agree, and since you mentioned the word, I'd like to talk about the 'sir' thing. We all know I'm a captain. With that and fifty piastres, you might be able to get a cup of Vietnamese coffee. My rank doesn't make me anything special—or help me know the best way to do things or make me right all the time.

"I'm just like you. I know a few things, and I'm learning all the time. Lately, I've been learning a lot about myself. For example, even though I've just arrived, I've learned that my job isn't to play the all-knowing captain every waking moment. I've also understood we're all in this together, and I'm a part of this team just like each of you—no better, no different.

"But let's be clear, when it's required, I'll be a traditional 'sir.' The rest of the time, particularly while we're out in the field, I want us to operate in a little more relaxed way. How about you just call me JB?"

Heads nodded, and one smart ass piped up, "Yes, sir, JB!"—prompting chuckles all around and a sideways look from Jack.

Jack waited for the chuckles to die out before he picked up the narrative again. "The way I see it, one of my most important responsibilities is paying attention—to be alert to what's going on with each of you and between all of us—and call it like I see it, straight up, no BS attached. The same thing applies to each of you too.

"The idea of calling it like you see it reminds me of one of the biggest lessons I learned in Ranger School, which was about communicating. I had more than one experience there where I was in the dark about what the hell was going on in the missions I was on. Thank God they weren't the real thing, or a lot of people wouldn't have made it.

"During one particular incident, I swore that once I was in a unit with real soldiers like you, I'd make sure that everybody got information about what would likely affect them. I'll make the same promise to you right now. I'll never order or ask you to do anything without some kind of explanation. Fair?"

"Yes, JB."

"While I'm on the lessons I learned in Ranger School, I want to mention a three-word phrase that to me sums up what working together means and how to do it. The phrase is 'cooperate and graduate.' The whole Ranger course is designed to teach it.

"Sure, the school teaches other subjects and skills too—the ones you hear about, such as testing your physical and mental limits and teaching you about hand-to-hand combat, survival, patrolling, mountain climbing, and others. None of them though, compares to what you learn about the importance of cooperation.

"Working together was drilled into our heads, and the guys who didn't take it seriously and didn't demonstrate they understood it didn't graduate. It was that serious. 'Cooperate and graduate' was my number-one takeaway from those nine hellish weeks. How we apply it here will determine whether—and how—we get through what lies ahead.

"Questions?" No one spoke.

"Okay," Jack responded. "One more thing and then I'll shut up. Small things can make a big difference. Where we're headed, doing what we're going to be doing, our attention to the details can save our lives or get us killed. So we all need to sweat the small stuff. No detail, no intuition, nothing is too small to mention. Make sense?"

With that, Jack took a deep breath and a swig of his beer and sat back, making eye contact with each man around the table. He wondered, "Did I get through to them, or was I just beating my gums?"

He didn't have to wait long for the answer. One by one, the men began to chime in, reiterating and supporting Jack's points, adding their own spin. They spoke candidly about themselves and their backgrounds, and mirroring Jack, they each talked about what working together meant to them. As they did, the foundations of the team that would sustain them were being laid.

The session lasted most of the night. More beers were drunk—a lot more. Everyone opened up about their fears, laughed, shared war stories, and discussed their expectations for one another and for Jack. By the time the first light of dawn crept in through the windows, a sense of soldierly camaraderie had settled over the group. They had made a solid beginning, knowing it wouldn't be the last sleepless night they would spend together.

# 4 Getting from Me to We

Pay attention to right now. Sweat the small stuff. Care about the people you're with. Work, learn, and lead together like your life depends on it.

—Jack Barrett

*Vietnam. 1971 and 1972.*

The lessons that Jack shared with his unit didn't come easily to him. In chapter 1, he faced a crucial situation that left him with few alternatives but to rely on himself and the soldiers he'd be leading. They all shared the metaphorical map, and with it, working together, they forged their own new trail through the challenges of leading in Vietnam.

Decades later, Robert E. Quinn, professor emeritus at the University of Michigan, described the phenomenon Jack and his team experienced. He said that its occurrence arises in moments of intense focus and commitment to a goal, marked by openness to others' influence. He called it "entering the fundamental state of leadership."[1]

The openness Quinn speaks about proved to be a lifeline for Jack and his team. They all understood—and agreed—that success wasn't just about accomplishing their assigned mission; it was equally about doing everything in their power to get everyone home safely. These two outcomes weren't mutually exclusive. In fact, they were complementary.

To succeed, Jack and his team relied on something none of them could have named at the time: interdependence. They simply called it working together. The key was that, almost instinctively, Jack involved his soldiers in decisions that affected them—decisions that in combat encompassed nearly everything. He taught them what he knew, and in return, they educated him.

This mutual reliance was not only practical but literally a matter of life and death. No single person could see the full picture or make the right decisions alone. Together, Jack and his soldiers built a team where every person mattered, everyone contributed, and everyone shared a stake in the mission's success.

When asked how they survived one of the most dangerous phases of the war, Jack's answer is always the same: "We learned how to work and lead together like our lives depended on it."

The team's explanation was pithier: "We figured out how to take it from 'me' to 'we.'"

You and your team can make this same shift by being serious about taking two giant-size steps:

1. Break free from the illusion that leadership has anything to do with authoritarian control, unquestioning obedience, and narrow self-interest.
2. Embrace what it's actually about, which is authenticity, shared purpose, voluntary commitment, and mutual influence.

This transformation from illusion to reality is more than just a philosophical shift; it's a practical reimagining of what leadership looks like in action.

Beginning with his own aha moment during his first twenty-four hours in Vietnam, Jack's story centers on how he and his team learned to work together to survive in a war zone. While your circumstances are likely different, your success and livelihood still hinge on your ability to collaborate effectively. This alone makes it worth your while to explore what it takes to operate from the Actual Leadership column in table 2.1 and help your team make the move from *me* to *we*.

Let's begin your own journey of team collaboration with figure 4.1, the dependence-interdependence road map, which is categorically different from the one Jack's military science professor in college referred to.[2]

Notice how the map runs from left to right—from dependence through independence—and onward to interdependence. Each step reflects a distinct mindset and corresponding behaviors that affect not only your team but also the broader interactions you have with others at work and beyond.

As you read the following descriptions of these steps, reflect on how your own experience aligns with, deviates from, or challenges these patterns. We'd love to hear your thoughts as well as about what you've learned from your own experience. Please get in touch at www.ccla-co.com.

## DEPENDENCE

Dependence occurs when someone's ability to act, think, or decide is tethered to another, such as a child who relies on a parent, a patient on a doctor, or soldiers on a military officer with a map.

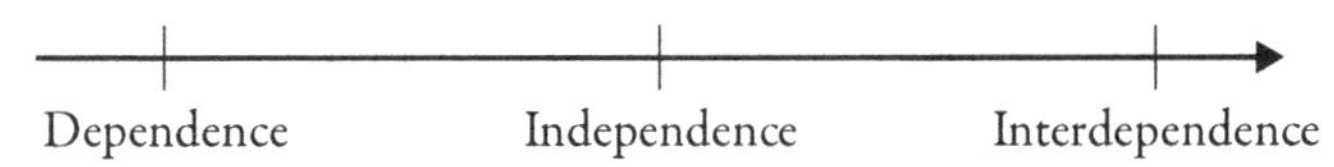


**FIGURE 4.1. THE DEPENDENCE-INTERDEPENDENCE ROADMAP**

Dependence is a completely natural part of the human experience. People everywhere lean on one another. You and your team rely on one another. Even CEOs depend on their boards of directors and other advisers.

Sometimes, however, dependence can become the sole way of functioning, stifling courage, creativity, and progress. People stop speaking out or sharing ideas, fearing repercussions and fostering toxic "just-do-what-you're-told" cultures that inevitably fail. Dependence is a trickster that might initially feel like a safe space for you, but its long-term effects are often crippling.

Consider the kind of workplace where employees are afraid to speak up because every decision must pass through an unapproachable manager. Over time, the team becomes stagnant, producing uninspired work and missing opportunities for innovation. Eventually, as Gallup has recently reported, in these situations, people fall into and become ensnared in the grip of what it labels "the Great Detachment."[3]

Unable to find suitable alternative employment, people lose hope and resign themselves to the status quo, becoming further victimized by ineffective leadership and the pervasive absence of meaningful connection. You can see where a steady diet of this might lead.

Reflecting on his time in the army, Jack recalls how easy it was to blame "those bastards up at higher headquarters" for every problem—whether warranted or not. This behavior, rooted in feelings of dependency and powerlessness, led to a wide range of dangerous incidents that culminated in deadly fragging attacks on leaders that were common.

Unfortunately, overreliance on dependency is still alive and well today—in workplaces, schools, and communities where it remains the default—not because it's the best choice. It's not. Dependence often persists because leaders are afraid of what will happen if their team members become independent, don't know how to get a team of independent people to work together, and can't envision the benefits of independence and where it can lead if properly guided.

The good news is that every one of these concerns can be addressed and alleviated by understanding and following the dependence-interdependence road map, whose next milepost is independence.

## INDEPENDENCE

Learning how to become independent is one of the most significant lessons any of us ever learn. Think about how, as a child, you were dependent on your parents or guardians.

Reflect for a minute on the process of gaining your independence and becoming the person you are today. You may have been fortunate enough to learn how to be independent early in your life.

Others, however, may not have been so lucky. Many enter adulthood in the same state of dependence they've known all their lives. Some may end up on your team. If that happens, it's up to you to meet them where they are and carefully begin introducing them to the pleasures and pitfalls of independence.

For many people—maybe most—independence means freedom from dependence on and control by others. It means being left alone to act without interference.

While these statements are true, they miss an important point: in the best of cases, independence can become people's first step toward learning how to work interdependently with others, which is one of the hallmarks of a healthy and well-balanced adult life—and arguably one of its goals.

This is where you come in. As a leader, one of the most consequential actions you can take is to encourage and help your team become more independent. Here's why.

Before most people can truly appreciate the benefits of working together, they must learn to work through the challenges of independence—the remoteness of making decisions alone, managing everything themselves, and confronting isolation. Your guidance and support are key to ensuring the lessons inherent in this process are both learned and ingrained. You can help by offering insights, making observations, asking thoughtful questions, listening attentively, and even sharing stories.

One of our favorite stories comes from the ancient Greek storyteller Aesop. His well-known fable "The Four Oxen and the Lion" carries a message that's relevant to the topic at hand.[4]

Once upon a time, a lion prowled a field where four oxen grazed. As lions are accustomed to doing, he attacked them when he was hungry. But whenever the lion came near, the oxen turned their tails to one another, so no matter how he approached, the beast was always met by a set of horns.

After years of fending off repeated attacks, the oxen began quarreling about which one was the best defender. As they argued, they wandered off to different parts of the pasture alone. This was exactly what the lion had been waiting for, and one by one, he attacked and ate them all—such are the eventual wages of independence.

By following the dependence-interdependence road map, you can help others not only achieve the goal of independence, but also meet the prerequisite for making one of the most enriching and rewarding—and yet least well-understood—life passages they'll ever experience: becoming the agents of their own futures.

## Becoming the Agent of Your Own Future

What exactly does it mean to become the agent of your own future? Why do so few people, leaders included, know about it? And why, if we do, aren't we talking more about it and actively teaching it?

Agency is the ability to act autonomously and with purpose and to make meaningful decisions that shape outcomes. It isn't simply doing things on your own; it's having the confidence, skills, and freedom to act in ways that align with your goals and values, and, in the best of cases, those of your organization.

Agency is the bridge over the troubled water that separates the helplessness of dependence and the exhilaration of interdependence shown in figure 4.2. You have a primary role in designing and building it as well as encouraging people to walk across it.

Here are some ideas for helping your team and others work toward and achieve personal agency:

- Create safe environments that encourage exploration beyond the boundaries of individuals' comfort zones.
- Assign challenging tasks that stretch people's capabilities.
- Celebrate effort and initiative, regardless of whether the outcome is perfect.
- Model courage by taking risks and sharing lessons you learned from your own failures.

These actions and others like them build trust and confidence, helping people discover their potential and build resilience. Agency doesn't diminish teamwork—it strengthens it by creating a culture where everyone can contribute their own best efforts.

Sadly, not everyone sees it this way, so a word to the wise: encouraging and sponsoring people's personal agency can inadvertently trigger

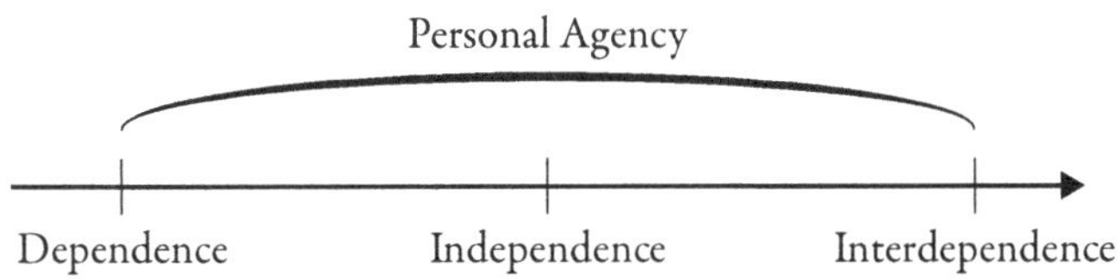


**FIGURE 4.2. PERSONAL AGENCY: A BRIDGE OVER TROUBLED WATER**

the immune systems of any champions of the command-and-control leadership approach in your proximity.

## Triggering the Command-and-Control Immune System

Command-and-control leadership thrives on dependency and subservience. Those who seek to promote their own or others' independence—let alone personal agency—risk intense scrutiny and even retaliation.

Professor Robert Quinn frames this dilemma as a choice: embrace "deep organizational—or even personal—change" or accept the status quo, which leads to what he calls "slow death."[5] What can you do in this situation? Quinn outlines three options:

- Keep quiet and accept the status quo—what he terms the "peace and pay option."
- Plan an "active exit," to leave the organization for a better fit.
- Courageously pursue "deep change."

You're only a few chapters into this book, but we'll wager that you already know where we come down. Here are some ideas about how you might move forward with the "deep change" option:

- Start with low risk, high return experiments involving independence and working together to show tangible benefits.
- Gather facts and data that point to the fact that making the journey from dependence to interdependence boosts measurable gains in metrics that leaders above you pay attention to, such as engagement, productivity, and retention.
- Ask people, including some of the command-and-control types, if they've ever found any benefits to collaboration. Ask them to tell you their stories.

The point is, don't give up. Keep pushing forward toward interdependence. That's how you can make a real contribution to the greater good.

As we mentioned at the outset, we'll return often to the interrelated themes of personal agency, collaboration, craft, and co-creation that are the crux of actual leadership.

With this in mind, let's explore the final stop on the road map, the way of working that Jack and his team couldn't name—interdependence.

## INTERDEPENDENCE

Team performance coach Dr. Ruth Wageman opines that interdependence is "the extent to which team members work collectively, affect, and are affected by others."[6] The dictionary says that it's "the state of being dependent on one another."[7]

Regardless of how you think about or define it, mutual dependence is a reality we all share. It's also one we often fail to sufficiently recognize or act on in ways that might enhance our ability to live and work together more effectively.

Based on our experience, we'd offer several reasons for this, including that many people labor under the yoke of dependence, never having worked in a truly independent or interdependent team. Or they embrace independence as a life goal because they were taught from an early age that it's synonymous with a fulfilling life—the place where they believe they'll find and enjoy the elusive state called freedom. Some may believe that relying on others means relinquishing control.

Regardless of the reason, it's this shortsightedness that makes it challenging to convince your team of independent agents—who, by the way, you encouraged—that they can amplify the impact of their freedom and personal power by giving some of it away.

There's no sugarcoating it: inspiring people to move toward interdependence is one of the most challenging leadership tests you'll ever face. It requires you to be a knowledgeable guide, a masterful teacher, and a patient communicator. Here are some ideas about how you might proceed:

- Imagine that you're guiding your team through a short action-learning workshop. First, you invite them to join you in taking the "human knot challenge."[8]

  This activity is simple and fun to do, and the discussion part that follows is easy to customize to fit your needs. You don't need any materials—just you and the members of your team. Here's how to go about it:
  - Form a tight circle with everyone standing shoulder to shoulder.
  - Each person grabs two different hands across the circle.
  - Without letting go, all participants work together to untangle themselves and form a complete circle.
- After completing the challenge, lead a discussion about what happened, how people reacted, and what they learned. Once this discussion is completed and you've demonstrated and discussed the idea of interdependence, the next step is to engage the team in imagining, or brainstorming, as many advantages of working together interdependently as possible. Here are a few questions to get started:
  - How might we leverage each other's strengths to realize and take advantage of more opportunities?
  - What could we achieve by combining our talents, like soloists do when they perform with others in an orchestra?
  - What can we learn from one another by working interdependently?
- Remind team members of the power of interdependence through mottoes. We once worked with a CEO who used every opportunity—some he conjured out of thin air—to communicate the

> kind of "one company culture" he sought to build, specifically focused on interdependence.
>
> He repeatedly referred to the Three Musketeers' motto—"One for all and all for one"—and the lyrics of the Bob Marley and the Wailers track "One Love," proving that leaders can use lots of ways to get the message about interdependence through to their people. Let's face it, if you can use the respective genius of a mixed-race French playwright along with the words of a Jamaican reggae singer—born more than a century apart—to communicate the interconnectedness of the human experience, why not? What else might you be able to dream up to get people's attention? The possibilities are limited only by your imagination.

By fostering an awareness of what interdependence is and isn't, its benefits, and the practical steps toward it, you can help your team build stronger working relationships and unlock new levels of productivity and creativity that can come only from working as a cohesive, interdependent unit.

There's no substitute for engaging your team in discussions about dependence, independence, and interdependence, teaching and learning with them about the things all of you need to know and do as you take your first tentative steps toward cooperation, collaboration, and beyond.

## A WORD ABOUT COOPERATION AND COLLABORATION

At first glance, collaboration and cooperation may seem similar, but the distinction between them lies in the depth of interaction and shared effort involved:

- Cooperation involves people working alongside each other, contributing individually toward a common goal, often with minimal coordination. People all do their part, but they may not engage deeply with one another's work. Cooperation is more about the division of tasks than shared problem-solving.
- Collaboration, on the other hand, goes deeper, requiring a more integrated effort. In collaboration, people work together actively, pooling resources, ideas, and expertise to achieve a common goal. It's characterized by higher levels of communication, mutual influence, and the blending of ideas to create something new or innovative.

In short, cooperation is about working in parallel with others, while collaboration weaves individuals' contributions together to create something greater than the sum of its parts. Recognizing these distinctions is the first step. The next is understanding how your own experiences, both as a team member and a leader, contribute to—or detract from—your encouragement of cooperation and collaboration.

## REFLECTING ON YOUR TEAM EXPERIENCES

Before we move ahead, take a moment to reflect on how your own experiences in teams have shaped your approach to teamwork. Here are a few questions to guide you:

- Questions about your experiences as a member of a team:
    - Where along the dependence-interdependence road map did teams you were part of operate?
    - What lessons, if any, did you take away from those experiences?
    - How have these lessons shaped your leadership approach?

- Questions about your experiences as the leader of a team:
    - Where would you place the teams you've led along the path between dependence and interdependence?
    - Were some teams further along than others? If so, what were the reasons?
    - If you're leading a team today, do people depend on you to handle things? Do they operate more independently? Or would you describe their way of working together as similar to the "all for one, and one for all" style of the Three Musketeers?
    - What would your team members say if you asked them these same questions?

Stepping back to reflect on your own experiences—as both a team member and a leader—can offer valuable insights. Similarly, engaging your team in the same type of exploration can serve as the first step in guiding them toward deeper collaboration and interdependence.

We encourage you to use these ideas as the basis for developing your own unique approach to, as Jaques and Clement say, "getting others to move along together with you, and with each other, with competence and full commitment, to achieve a goal."[9]

Chapters 3 and 4 debunk common leadership myths—such as the idea that leaders must have all the answers or follow a prescribed path—and reveal what leadership truly involves. While these insights are powerful, they aren't sufficient on their own. Their real value lies in how they're applied.

Your next steps are to identify how you can integrate these insights into your daily work and then implement them with the skill and intentionality of a true craftsperson.

# EXTRAS: CHAPTERS 3 AND 4

## Chapters 3 and 4 Summary

- Jack Barrett's time in Vietnam demonstrated that leadership begins with paying attention, caring for, and being open to learning from the people you work with. These lessons are as relevant today as they were in Jack's day.
- The dependence-interdependence road map illustrates that genuine teamwork, embodying the spirit of "we, us, ours" requires moving beyond the mentalities of "they, them, theirs" and "I, me, mine."
- Dependence occurs when someone's ability to act, think, or decide is tethered to another, such as a child who relies on a parent or a patient on a doctor.
- Many people view independence as freedom from dependence on and control by others. It means being left alone to act without interference.
- While these statements about independence are true, they miss an important fact: that independence can also be people's first step toward learning how to work *interdependently* with others.
- As your team members begin to move from dependence to independence and onward toward interdependence, use your influence as a leader to encourage and help them develop a sense of their own personal power.
- This sense of personal power is more formally known as *personal agency,* which is the self-directed capacity to make decisions, take action, and take responsibility for the outcomes.
- Personal agency isn't something you do or give to others. And it most definitely is not so-called empowerment. It's something you teach them about, facilitate, and foster.

- Helping people become agents of their own futures is one of the most important contributions you can make to your team and others around you.

One day, looking back on your career and accomplishments, you may find that you're most proud of helping instill personal agency in others. It's that significant.

## How to Use the Information in Chapters 3 and 4

Use an upcoming team meeting to discuss the concept of working together. Let team members know in advance that this will be the focus, and ask them to reflect on and share what working together means to them personally.[10]

Reference the dependence-interdependence road map to guide the discussion, and ask your team the following questions:

- Where along the path toward interdependence do you think we are as a team today?
- What specific behaviors can you point to that support your opinion? Please be specific.
- Why is our current location on the road map important?
- What specific actions should we take as a team to move closer to working together interdependently?

Verse 10, *Tao Te Ching*

By patience the animal spirits can be disciplined.
By self-control one can unify the character.
By close attention to the will, compelling gentleness,
one can become like a little child.

By purifying the subconscious desires
one may be without fault.
In ruling his country, if the wise magistrate
loves his people, he can avoid compulsion.
In measuring out rewards, the wise magistrate will
act like a mother bird.
While sharply penetrating into every corner,
he may appear to be unsuspecting.
While quickening and feeding his people,
he will be producing but not without pride of ownership.
He will benefit but without claim of reward.
He will persuade, but not compel by force.
This is *Te,* the profoundest virtue.

## Final Thoughts

Small things often make a big difference. In the one hundred-meter sprint, the margin between Olympic gold and silver can be just 0.03 seconds—the blink of an eye.[11] Michael Phelps famously won the one hundred-meter butterfly at the 2008 Olympics by 0.01 seconds, or the difference of a fingertip.[12]

Given such tiny margins, how would you approach making improvements in how you lead? Would you work harder, practice more, or hire a coach? Maybe you would do all of these and more. But none of them would make a difference if you didn't focus on the smallest details you needed to improve.

Just as in Olympic competitions, the smallest adjustments in how you lead can be the difference between good and great. What are the small parts of your leadership approach? Which ones are you overlooking? Which ones could you focus more on to improve? Even the tiniest adjustments can have a profound effect.

This is the mindset of a craftsperson.

# 5 The Right Things the Right Way

Whatsoever thy hand findeth to do, do it with thy might;
for there is no work, nor device, nor knowledge,
nor wisdom, in the grave, whither thou goest.

—Ecclesiastes 9:10

*Fort Lewis, Washington. 1974.*

After returning from the war, Jack was still haunted by it. Despite doing his job admirably, earning medals along the way, and ensuring that he and his soldiers made it home safely, he couldn't shake off the cloying feeling of the senselessness of it all. He'd lost his innocence along with any illusions that there was anything "right" about war at all, particularly for the reasons and the way it was waged in Southeast Asia.

Today, with more willingness to listen, ask questions, and understand the experiences people have in war or other traumatic events, society is better able to identify and understand a whole panoply of conditions—ranging from posttraumatic stress disorder to depression, anxiety disorders, substance abuse, survivor's guilt, and moral injury. But in the early 1970s, people hadn't found a name for the burden that

Jack and tens of thousands of other veterans carried when they returned home and did their best to reenter their former, so-called normal lives.

That's what Jack was mostly still trying unsuccessfully to do when, under protest, nearly two years later, he took his seat in the Officers' Club Ballroom at Fort Lewis, Washington. Under direct orders, he and the rest of the officers of the US Army's Ninth Infantry Division Artillery were there to hear remarks from their new commanding officer, Colonel James P. Forrest.

Jack glanced out at the serene scene beyond the ballroom's floor-to-ceiling window. The emerald hills, dotted with western red cedars and Douglas firs, shimmered with an almost unreal beauty—a perfection that only deepened the stark, colorless cynicism churning within him.

His expectations for the new colonel were about as low as they could get. Jack had already relegated him to being just another prototypical hard-assed army careerist—like the ones he'd come across in Vietnam, where he learned that disappointment in his superiors was about the only thing he could count on.

After the briefest of introductions by his adjutant, Colonel Forrest took the stage. Jack felt the familiar knot of suspicion and distrust tighten in his stomach. But as Forrest started to speak, Jack noted his calm tone, matter-of-fact delivery, and almost casual confidence.

"Good afternoon, ladies and gentlemen. It's good to be with you today. I'm sure you're wondering who I am and what I'm all about, so I'll get straight to it. The most important thing you need to know about me is that I'm a stickler for doing the right things the right way. Let me give you an example."

As the colonel paused before he continued, something unusual happened: Jack's knot relaxed a little.

"Years ago, while we were in Germany, my wife, Nancy, and I bought a new Mercedes sedan with a diesel engine. We still own it and drive it every day. I drove it here from my office. It has over three hundred fifty thousand miles on the odometer, and we expect to put a good many more on it before it needs any serious maintenance.

"When people see the car and hear about the mileage, they're amazed. 'Wow,' they say. 'That's a lot of miles. What's the secret of your success?'

"It's this: maintaining a diesel engine depends largely on how it's started and how it's shut down. It might surprise you to hear that there's a proper way to do both.

"I tell you this story because it reflects one of my core philosophical beliefs. Success is about doing the right things the right way. It holds true for everything you do, including how you lead soldiers. I call it my failsafe philosophy: do the right things the right way, and you won't fail." Forrest paused, letting the room absorb the connection. (We've included figure 5.1, which lays out Forrest's philosophy in a graph.)

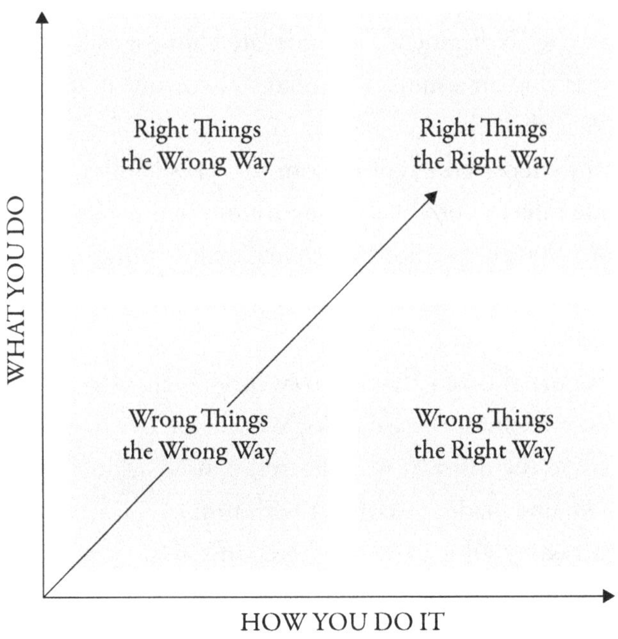


**FIGURE 5.1. THE RIGHT THINGS THE RIGHT WAY**

The story about the meticulously maintained Mercedes caught Jack's attention. He could almost hear the engine purr in his mind, a stark contrast to the grinding machinery of war that still haunted his dreams. The tension in the room shifted as the audience leaned in, Forrest's voice steady and deliberate, filling the space as he continued.

Forrest's words were practical almost to a fault, and Jack found himself nodding in agreement. But suddenly, he was back in Tây Ninh Province, where doing things the "right way" had always been a murky concept, especially in the jungle, where survival often meant bending or breaking rules that didn't make sense on the ground.

Then, almost as fast, he was in Germany before the war, listening to the wisdom of his boss, Paul Lustig, who was fond of saying, "Nothing changes if nothing changes."

Jack spoke silently to the new colonel, almost as if trying to communicate with him telepathically: "So, Colonel, what specifically is going to change here with you?" The truth was, Jack expected the answer was going to be "Not much." Seconds later, almost as if on cue, Forrest resumed speaking on a subject familiar to everyone in the room. "Here it comes," Jack thought.

"I recently received a report from the MPs [military police] about the roadside safety spot checks they routinely do around the post. As you're aware, these inspections are to make sure military vehicles are safe and well maintained." Groans from the audience indicated they were aware indeed.

"The report showed that over twenty-seven of our vehicles were stopped last month for these checks. Would you like to guess how many of them passed the inspections?" Forrest paused again and scanned the audience. No one made eye contact with him.

"Embarrassingly for everyone here, only nine of our twenty-seven vehicles passed. That's a failure rate of 67 percent. Put another way, the MPs permitted only one out of every three of our vehicles to be driven away from their inspection sites. The others were declared unsafe to drive. They had to be towed back to their motor pools at huge extra expenditures of time, money, and personnel.

"Clearly, the right things are not being done the right way. This kind of performance is unacceptable. New standards are required. Therefore, effective immediately, the new division artillery standard for passing MP roadside spot checks is . . ."

Jack's stomach churned with the memory of past failures, of missions that had gone sideways because of the impossible demands from superiors. He braced himself for the inevitable order, the one that would push everyone in the room to the breaking point.

"Effective immediately," Forrest said, his voice unwavering, "the new roadside spot check standard for our organization is . . . 50 percent."

Jack's heart skipped a beat. Only 50 percent? His mind whirred, caught between disbelief and a flicker of hope. This wasn't the army he knew, where perfection was demanded at any cost. A goal of 50 percent was reasonable. It was achievable. And it was . . . human.

Jack's friend and colleague Captain Pat Malone leaned over, whispering, "What do you think, Jack? Is this guy for real?"

Jack didn't answer immediately. His thoughts were too jumbled, memories of Vietnam crashing against the unexpected rationality of Forrest's approach. Could this new colonel truly be different? Was it possible that someone up the chain of command understood the toll that the absurd, relentless pressure on results at any cost was taking?

That evening over dinner, Jack's wife asked him a question that mirrored his own doubts. "Do you think this new CO is the genuine article?"

Jack stared at the table, his fork tracing patterns in his mashed potatoes. "I'm not sure," he replied, the words heavy. But something had shifted in him—something small and fragile yet undeniably present. "But I think . . . maybe." As they sat in silence, Jack couldn't shake the feeling that a change was coming. For the first time in a long while, he felt something other than disillusionment. It was hope—tenuous and uncertain—but it was hope nonetheless.

# 6 Leading with Craft

Perhaps we're entering a new age of craftsmanship, one where we can see craft in the way a new business is devised, a sale is made or a website is coded. A craftsperson might be particularly talented and connected in the way she deals with clients, or be able to meet deadlines with alacrity. Just because it's not in a crafts fair doesn't mean it didn't demand craft.

—Seth Godin

*Fort Lewis, Washington. 1974, a few weeks later.*

Jack and the other officers of the division artillery knew within a few weeks after Colonel Forrest arrived that he was different. He wasn't just authoritative—he was precise, thoughtful, and deliberate. They could plainly see that he led with the skill and care of a craftsman, aiming to shape not just strategies and results but also people.

Forrest embodied leadership as craft by setting and communicating realistic goals, weaving compelling stories to convey key points, and emphasizing doing the right things the right way—not just his way or the army's way. His leadership created a culture of rationality, growth, and development, all of which exemplified what Seth Godin describes as the "new age of craftsmanship."[1]

## EXPANDING THE DEFINITION OF CRAFT INTO TODAY

Traditionally, craft has been defined as the work of skilled artisans using materials like wood, clay, glass, or metal to create something of beauty by hand. However, in today's world, the concept of craft has expanded beyond these materials to encompass expertise in many fields—whether you're working with wood, words, bits and bytes, or protein and produce, craft and craftwork are about the intentional and masterful application of skill to create something meaningful, enduring, and well made. Let's take a dive deeper into the nature of craft and craftwork in the twenty-first century.

Today, the concept of craft encompasses ideas from fields too numerous to mention, so we'll focus on two of the most unique and fascinating. The first comes from Judith Weir, CBE, Master of the King's Music, and official composer to King Charles III. Weir describes craft as "the outcome of numerous small actions carried out with discipline."[2]

Similarly, American singer, songwriter, and writer Rosanne Cash, daughter of country music superstar Johnny Cash, believes that "craft is the dovetailing of discipline and imagination, dedication and inspiration. When those spiral around each other, and serious attention is given over to that alchemy, then one's craft can be realized."[3]

Craft and craftwork have been described in numerous ways, many focusing on their nature and practice. Almost without exception, they all converge on the idea that they are expressions of the human spirit, embodying the idea "This is who I am and what I can achieve in my medium."

This emerging perspective broadens the definition of craft to include working with people. Exceptional educators, expert therapists, and caring clergy to name a few, all engage in what we like to call "people-crafting." You can do this as well, and nowhere is the opportunity to develop others and help them become all they can be more prevalent or impactful than in your work as a leader.

As a leader, the medium you work in is people—their hearts, minds, and spirits, the value of which easily surpasses even the rarest and most precious of materials—gold, silver, and precious gemstones. By helping develop others toward their potential, you're shaping lives and livelihoods far into the future.

## CONNECTIONS BETWEEN CRAFT, CRAFTWORK, AND LEADERSHIP

As we researched the intricacies of craftwork for this book, we found intriguing parallels between artisanal skills and leadership. The more we studied the nuances of traditional craft, the more we saw these same principles in the Leadership Actually Model (defined in chapter 2), which emphasizes clear, thoughtful, and person-to-person leadership.

We interviewed a diverse group of craftspeople to see what we might learn. Our interviews included a potter, carpenter, public speaker, two physical therapists, and a writer and editor in the United States; an authority in garment product development and a boxing coach in Hong Kong; a leader in international education in Beijing; a bespoke jeweler and diamond trader in Singapore; a marketing executive specializing in brand formation in Thailand; an art gallery owner in London; and the owner of an international executive search agency in Spain.

These skilled professionals are neither celebrities nor household names. You're unlikely to find them in the pages of the *London Times* or on television. Though they come from different fields and far-flung corners of the world, their work shares a common thread: a commitment to their craft that mirrors the dedication to craftwork that leaders like you must cultivate in your own work with people.

## FIVE COMMON ATTRIBUTES OF CRAFTSPEOPLE

As we interviewed these craftspeople across their diverse fields, we uncovered five attributes that set them apart. These attributes—inspiration, commitment, attention to detail, perseverance, and continuous learning—are the building blocks of mastery in any field of work, including leading a team. Here's how they stack up.

### Inspiration

Inspiration is the spark that drives action, often leading to passion. Passion, in turn, can reignite inspiration, creating a virtuous cycle. Inspired individuals exhibit strong emotions and high energy, attracting others to their cause.

#### Selected Quotes about Inspiration

Here is what some of our interviewees said about inspiration:

- "Learning and teaching inspire me. They're my life's work. I do my best to pass this along to others."
- "My mentor cared about me and my development. He shared his experiences with me, which no amount of money can buy. The way he worked inspired me."
- "My cousin was a diamond trader in Sydney, Australia. I witnessed the unbelievable level of trust he was able to establish with his customers. It amazed and inspired me. I wanted to learn how to do the same thing and pass it along to others."
- "My first professional inspiration came from two physical therapists (PTs) I went to see at their clinic in Pennsylvania. They modeled physical therapy in a way that I wanted to learn. Today I teach the same methodology to my students."

### The Relationship between Inspiration and Leading with Craft

The relationship between inspiration and leading with craft is grounded in the practice of teaching and learning. Our interviews revealed that leaders who emphasize craftsmanship find great fulfillment in nurturing the growth of others, which is one of the six core pieces of skilled leadership knowledge in our model.

Craftspeople are often inspired by learning new techniques and passing them on to others. This tradition, which dates back to at least the Middle Ages when master craftspeople trained apprentices, continues to inspire a commitment to actively spreading knowledge and skills today. Watching others learn, grow, and succeed can be a profound source of inspiration for you. Consider people you've mentored. What inspiration have you drawn from their journeys? How can you continue to reach and influence others through the art of teaching and leading with craft?

## Commitment

Commitment is a pledge to persist and a promise to follow through even when the going gets tough.[4] Commitment involves intention, stick-to-it-iveness, and perseverance. Unlike inspiration, which typically arises from external sources, commitment originates from inside of you.

### Selected Quotes about Commitment

Here are some insights on commitment from our interviewees:

- "Committing to become a craftsperson means being willing to endure discomfort to improve."
- "In the practice of physical therapy, you have to be willing to give people what they need versus something off the shelf that

might be easier. People trust you with their well-being. Giving them less than your committed best borders on the unethical. It probably won't work anyway. Really helping often means choosing the road seldom taken."

## The Relationship between Commitment and Leading with Craft

Effective leaders commit deeply to not just their work but also their own personal growth and that of the members of their teams. Sometimes, the demands of leadership will seem overwhelming. Your agenda may be full to overflowing, discretionary time scarce, and the expectation for outstanding results relentless. In those moments, the thought of giving up on leadership can be tempting. Many of us have entertained such thoughts.

Crises of commitment are not uncommon. But with the right mindset and strategies, they can be navigated. So when one of these crises arises, what can you do?

The first thing that's useful is to pause, reflect, and take a deep look inside yourself. As you do, consider asking yourself some of these self-awareness questions:

- "What emotions am I experiencing, and why?"
- "What specifically is causing me to feel so overwhelmed?"
- "Is there a small, manageable step I can take to move forward?"
- "Where can I go to get help?"
- "Who can I call to think out loud with?"

After reflecting on these questions, you may still need some time and patience. Remember, as the old Roman proverb wisely says, "No one masters their craft the first day." In other words, hang in there and keep going.

## Attention to Detail

As Jack is fond of saying, attention to detail is about "paying attention to right now, sweating the small stuff, caring about the people you're with, working and learning together, and above all, leading like your life depends on it." More pointedly, however, it's the ability to focus on the specifics, intricacies, and finer points within a task, situation, or context. It involves being meticulous, observant, and precise to ensure the levels of accuracy and quality and end results you'll be proud of.

### Selected Quotes about Attention to Detail

Here are some select quotes from our interviewees on attention to detail:

- "Craftsmanship requires laser-like focus on the details."
- "Despite the pressure, my mentor always paid attention to us. She took the time to get to know us personally, and that made us want to work hard for her."
- "When I was a new physical therapy graduate, a friend told me that I would never be really good because I was too interested in the details of my patients' lives and stories. What I learned over time, however, is that's precisely the reason I *am* a good PT."

### The Relationship between Attention to Detail and Leading with Craft

Attention to detail builds trust. Whether you're hiring a new team member or managing a project, getting the details right is crucial. Reflect on the last time you paid close attention to detail in your work. What was the outcome?

People tend to trust others who pay attention to detail. At the Co-Creative Leadership Alliance, two of us worked together on a project to find, select, and hire the pilots and crew for a client's personal Bombardier business jet. It was a stressful project because we knew lives depended on our judgment.

You can probably guess our top selection criterion: attention to detail. Too little attention could endanger lives; too much might lead to inaction that could also have dire consequences. We looked for people with a level of attention to detail that was just right. It took us a while to find them, but we did. Perseverance, which is the next attribute on this list, was a key factor in our search.

## Perseverance

Perseverance is the ability and willingness to keep going despite challenges. Leadership, like craftwork, often requires pushing through difficult times. History is full of examples of perseverance and how it paid off. Although the actual source of the quote is uncertain, during the Blitz in World War II, Sir Winston Churchill is widely credited with saying, "If you're going through hell, keep going." Luckily for all of us, he did.

### Selected Quotes about Perseverance

Here are some insights about perseverance from our interviewees:

- "You have to persevere if your aim is to be a craftsperson. It's about never quitting until you get it right."
- "In physical therapy, physical and specialist skills are necessary but not nearly as important as the mental ones like perseverance, the courage to try new things, and continual learning."
- "To be a craftsperson, you have to persevere. You have to be a progressive perfectionist. You never quit until you get it right, and that comes from experimenting, shaping, molding, adjusting, and learning through trial and error."

- "If you want to understand perseverance, start training for an eight-round boxing match. Better yet, get in the ring and see what it's like to keep going when it's difficult to just keep your hands up to defend yourself, much less throw punches at your opponent."

### The Relationship between Perseverance and Leading with Craft

Many people interpret the word *perseverance* to mean slogging through or plodding on. Sometimes, it feels exactly like that, but if you persist—if you keep on keeping on—with what you're doing, you'll likely make progress even if you do so slowly. When you persevere, you model resolve, tenacity, and dedication for others to see. You're walking the talk, which is what leaders do. To gain insight on your own level of perseverance, ask yourself these questions:

- Where would you put yourself on a hypothetical perseverance scale, with one being low and five being high?
- What's an example in your work of when you or a team member persevered? What was the result? How did it pay off?
- If your immediate manager asked you to teach a class on perseverance, what would you talk about, and how would you go about it? What stories could you tell to make the idea of perseverance come alive?

## Continuous Learning

Continuous learning is the ongoing process of acquiring knowledge and skills. Just beneath the surface of master craftspeoples' elegant ease with which they appear to do their work, you'll discover one of the biggest secrets of their success. They work damned hard to keep learning and growing.

Craftspeople are curious, habitual tinkerers. They tweak this and fine-tune that in search of the next higher plane of their craft. They always seem to be in a state of excited discovery. Their enthusiasm is a byproduct of their sharp understanding that learning and the next new idea can come at any time from anywhere, often from the least expected sources. There's no substitute for staying ready to learn.

## Selected Quotes about Continuous Learning

Here are some of our favorite quotes about continuous learning from our interviewees:

- "I learn something new every day, and then I learn even more when I try to apply it."
- "Becoming a craftsperson is about continually relearning how to use your mind to plan what your hands produce."
- "People may think they can learn it all very quickly. I'm into twenty-odd years of my work, and I am still learning. There is always something for me to learn as long as my goal is to improve myself and my skills."
- "When you learn a craft, the craft mixes with who you are and vice versa. It's almost as if you become one of the tools in your own toolbox."
- "My love of studying and learning sustains me. I learn, if for no other reason, simply for learning's sake. I can feel myself declining physically, but cognitively, I'm still able to study, learn, and function. My love of learning underpins everything I do and everything I am."
- "I've been in business for forty-three years. I've learned that things don't always go smoothly. Sometimes I make a sale, and a customer promises to pay but doesn't. Sometimes a person will return a piece after it's been worn for two years, saying it has a

defect. I make adjustments, but if they're still not happy, I buy the piece back. I've had to learn all of this along the way. I learn something new every single day."

### The Relationship between Continuous Learning and Leading with Craft

Learning to lead with craft is an opportunity to take advantage of learning that never stops. The curriculum of study is extensive. Its subjects range from the ordinary to the transformative—from the latest best practices to the ever-fluid interpersonal processes of your team.

Leaders who embrace continuous learning are always ready to adapt and grow. They see every experience—whether positive or negative—as an opportunity to learn.

Reflection is a useful and rewarding individual and team practice, particularly when it's focused on learning. Get into the regular practice of asking yourself at the end of each day what you learned. Do the same with your team once a week or so. We like the structure provided by three simple questions:

- "What happened today or this week?"
- "How did I react or feel about it?"
- "What did I learn?"

## WHY YOU SHOULD CONSIDER LEADING YOUR PROFESSIONAL CRAFT

In his book *Personality and the Fate of Organizations,* psychologist Robert Hogan says, "The most important psychological task of adulthood involves developing a story about one's life that makes sense of the past and paints a picture of the future. It's like developing a vision statement for one's career: This is what I stand for and this is why I stand for it."[5]

Craftsmanship is among the most valuable principles a leader can champion. This is particularly true today when craft is no longer limited to the traditional fields of art or artisanal work. Leading can and should be approached with the same level of care, intention, and mastery. The five attributes we uncovered from our interviews—inspiration, commitment, attention to detail, perseverance, and continuous learning—are the foundational elements of any craft. They also lie at the heart of exemplary leadership.

When you harness the power of inspiration, you ignite passion and energy within not only yourself but also those around you. Commitment drives you to stay the course through challenging circumstances, while attention to detail helps you build trust and ensure excellence. Through perseverance, you model resilience and resolve, showing your team that progress comes from persistence. And by embracing continuous learning, you stay adaptable and open to new insights, and you enable your team to grow alongside you, fostering a culture of shared development and innovation.

Much like how craftspeople dedicate time and energy to honing their skills, you must be equally resolute and committed to developing your craft. Craftsmanship isn't just about making objects; it's about making a difference. By committing to the craft of leadership, you can shape lives, build trust, and make a difference that matters. Here are a few questions to reflect on as we prepare to rejoin Jack on the next momentous step in his journey:

- What have you spent years perfecting?
- What makes your leadership unique?
- What specific actions can you take to elevate your leadership to the next level of craft?

Ultimately, leadership as craft is about more than managing people or achieving short-term results. It's about shaping lives, fostering growth, and leaving a legacy of excellence. The true art of leadership lies in your ability to blend skill, heart, and purpose in ways that transform both yourself and those you lead.

## EXTRAS: CHAPTERS 5 AND 6

### Chapters 5 and 6 Summary

- Back from the war after nearly two years, Jack continued to struggle with its emotional aftermath. He'd been severely disillusioned by his perception of the war's mismanagement by officers who treated their own soldiers, as well as their South Vietnamese allies, with disdain, falsified information to make themselves or their units look good, and made it their primary goal to win their next medal or commendation.
- Jack's perception of the army began to change when he attended a meeting run by Colonel James P. Forrest.
- Forrest shared a personal story about his diesel Mercedes, emphasizing the importance of proper maintenance and linking it to his leadership philosophy of "doing the right things the right way."
- He also introduced his fail-safe strategy: "If you do the right things the right way, you won't fail," causing Jack to listen more closely.
- But when Forrest mentioned the division artillery's recent substandard performance during roadside vehicle safety spot checks, Jack's cynicism returned. He knew what was coming. He'd heard it all before. Forrest's unexpected rationality in setting new performance goals, however, began to prompt Jack to reconsider his cynicism, opening a new door to a fragile hope for change.
- Jack's hopes were realized as Colonel Forrest's leadership philosophy took hold, resulting in concrete lessons that Jack and his

fellow officers learned from the example of a rational and human approach to leadership that Forrest provided. He practiced his profession as a craft years before anything other than artistic expression was considered craft-like.

- Today the definition of craftwork has broadened considerably, settling on one that asserts a craft is any work that requires the application and use of specialized knowledge and skills.
- The practice of leadership far exceeds this criterion, and leaders should treat their work as a craft.
- Leading with craft involves the intentional application and use of a defined leadership mindset and a small body of skilled leadership knowledge both leavened by a leader's personal sensibilities. Intertwined, these are aimed at "getting others to move along together with them, and with each other, with competence and full commitment, to achieve a goal."[6]
- Chapter 6 includes a series of interviews the authors conducted to determine the similarities between the work of craftspeople and that of leaders. Five attributes were found to be common to both: inspiration, commitment, attention to detail, perseverance, and continuous learning.

## How to Use the Information in Chapters 5 and 6

Following are five practical strategies drawn from our own experience that can help you weave craft into how you lead.

### Do It Scared

Remember when you learned to swim? The scariest part was letting go of the side of the pool. With your heart pounding, you released your grip and finally pushed off into the water.

While frightening, letting go of the side of the pool is something you have to do if your goal is to swim the two hundred-meter butterfly. Done sensibly, having the courage to make yourself vulnerable and face something that frightens you can open up new vistas of learning and growth. Look for opportunities to let go of the side of whatever pool you're in at the moment. Do whatever it is you want to do, even if you have to do it scared.

## Build Trust Rather than Create Suspicion

Eminent social and personality psychologist Robert Hogan opines in his 2007 book, *Personality and the Fate of Organizations*—a must-have on your leadership bookshelf—"The first question asked of leaders and prospective leaders is, can they be trusted not to abuse the privilege of authority?"[7]

Recognize that this question of trust is not only the first but a perpetual query in the minds of people you seek to lead. Answering it affirmatively through your words and deeds is one of the keys to leading successfully.

Here's a way to check in with yourself we learned from a conversation we had with Elliott Jaques: before you do or say something that involves other people, simply ask yourself, "Is what I'm about to do or say likely to build trust or create suspicion?" Let the answer that bubbles up from inside you inform and influence what you do next.

Integrating this simple little question into your leadership and interpersonal repertoire will help you build and maintain trust over time. It'll also make you a better leader and a better person in one fell swoop.

## Find the Right Teacher

A popular belief holds that when the student is ready, the teacher will appear. That's not true. You'll know when you're ready, and finding a teacher that fits you and your individual needs and wants is your responsibility.

This undertaking is important enough that you shouldn't leave it to chance. Nothing we know of will help you get better at leading more effectively than finding a teacher and getting some individualized feedback, advice, and instruction.

Look for a teacher with integrity, a leader who has wide experience but not necessarily someone with impressive academic credentials. The teacher you seek should be passionate, knowledgeable, and authentic. Once you find someone you think is a good fit for you, make contact and explain what you're after. Tell them you'd like to buy a day or two of their time to explore the possibility of working together in a teacher-learner relationship. This is often how it begins.

## Put Together a Constellation of Colleagues

The word *constellation* typically refers to a configuration of stars. We love this imagery. When used to describe a connected network of personal friends and colleagues, it conjures all sorts of fascinating possibilities. We imagine our own constellations of colleagues as webs of bright stars swirling slowly around us, available for advice or counsel or maybe just to lend an occasional ear.

Start building your constellation of collegial working relationships, and fill it with stars of your choice—from butchers to bakers to whomever, people who come from walks of life different from your own.

Choose people who have something valuable to teach that you want to learn, a unique perspective or a sharp insight. It's never too early or too late to seek out people you want in your constellation. Concentrate on quality, not quantity. Go after diversity of expertise and thought.

## Lift Your Game and Elevate the Level of Your Work

As a leader, you have more opportunities to positively affect people than almost anyone else in their lives. This alone is motivation enough to do everything you can to take what you do up a level by thinking bigger.

An example of what we mean by thinking bigger is a process we call *synthesizing*, which is one of the most useful ways for you to think bigger while you move toward higher and more effective levels of your work. Synthesizing involves the cultivation of the conscious habit of being on the lookout for the latest ideas, innovations, and best practices from the best thinkers everywhere so you can incorporate them into your work.[8]

Verse 45, *Tao Te Ching*

Extreme perfection seems imperfect,
its function is not exhausted.
Extreme fulfillment appears empty,
its function is not exercised.
Extreme straightness appears crooked;
great skill, clumsy;
great eloquence, stammering.
Motion conquers cold,
quietude conquers heat.
Not greatness but purity and clearness
are the world's standard.

## Final Thoughts

Jack's perspective on leadership shifted as a result of the authenticity with which Colonel Forrest led, moving him away from disillusionment and cynicism and toward a renewed sense of hope. As Forrest's philosophies took root and questions about the way he led were answered affirmatively, Jack and others started to see leadership as a craft requiring dedication, skill, and practice.

Unbeknownst to Colonel Forrest and Jack at the time, they were both on the threshold of their futures: one destined to become a four-star general and the other on the path of becoming not just a leader but a teacher—a role that would define his life. Their paths would cross again, but that's a story for another time.

In the next chapter, Jack will have one of those life-changing experiences that people talk about. This moment was truly transformational, raising his consciousness and redefining his understanding of both himself and his role as a leader.

What about you? We're willing to bet that you've had your own memorable leadership moments—whether it was something you achieved yourself or something you learned from another leader's actions. Think about the moments that shaped your growth and the lessons you've carried with you.

We'd love to hear about these moments that have shaped you, whether they were challenges you faced or lessons you learned from others. Share your story with us at www.ccla-co.com and become a part of the growing conversation about leadership as craft.

# PART 2

# Laying the Foundation to Lead

In part 1, we set the stage for leadership by exploring its three pillars: mindset, skilled knowledge, and personal sensibilities—all essential to practicing the Leadership Actually Model. We also introduced the perspective that leadership is as much a craft to you as art was to Picasso and music was to Mozart.

In part 2, we dive deeper into three core elements of skilled leadership knowledge, which comprise the foundation of effective leadership regardless of the particular approach you use. Specifically, we'll explore how to do the following:

- Understand and use the Content and Process Model.
- Improve your self-awareness.
- Turn information into effective communication.

As we delve into these elements, we'll emphasize the knowledge and skills required to apply and use them in ways that not only enhance how you lead but also how you can create a lasting impact in doing so.

Moving through part 2, we'll occasionally let Jack and his teachers take center stage by defining the leadership principles under discussion. As we do, think about how you might apply and use these core elements in your leadership role to help you lead with greater clarity and effectiveness.

# 7 Paradigm Shift

Education is a progressive discovery of our own ignorance.

—Will Durant

*US Army Organizational Effectiveness School. 1976.*

Subtle shades of the blue-gray Pacific sparkled in the offshore distance as morning broke peacefully over the quaint seaside village of Monterey, California. Low-hanging clouds of the marine layer moved slowly inland, enveloping fishing boats, wharves, and the disused traces of the once-bustling sardine factories immortalized in John Steinbeck's celebrated novel *Cannery Row.*

The big army base at Fort Ord, just a few miles north along the Pacific Coast Highway, stood in stark contrast. Here, the serenity of the coast gave way to a world of precise lines, purposeful regimentation, and the relentless buzz of soldierly life. The energy at Fort Ord was palpable, vibrating through the air. At this base, soldiers honed their skills with an intensity that some said was nothing less than the army rediscovering its "mojo" after the demoralizing war in Southeast Asia. The timing could not have been better.

In the wake of Vietnam, the army was embarking on a new era, one largely defined by its transition from a conscripted—involuntarily drafted—force to what was called the Modern Volunteer Army. Fort Ord was chosen as a testing ground for the ideas and innovations that the army envisioned would shape and revitalize its future.

Central to this vision was the army's new Organizational Effectiveness (OE) Program, an adaptation of the well-established field of organization development from the business world.

OE promised to be a game-changer—a comprehensive strategy aimed at revolutionizing the army's rigid, top-down leadership culture through inclusive, collaborative, and noncoercive ways of leading. Yet opinions varied. Some hailed OE as a bold, necessary shift that promised to address and heal deep fissures that had festered in the force for decades and come to a head in Vietnam.

Others, proponents of the old school army who enforced discipline through authority and fear saw OE as a dangerous paradigm shift that would challenge traditional ways of thinking about leadership and replace them with new, untested, and antithetical methods.

Understanding a paradigm shift intellectually is one thing; experiencing its jarring impact firsthand is another. The visible nervousness of a small cohort of thirty officers, including Captain Jack Barrett, made that impact plain. They'd been selected to attend one of the army's first sixteen-week OE training courses at Fort Ord.

Each had gone all in on a very big bet. They'd wagered their army careers on a one-way ticket into the unknown. No one knew whether OE would work in an organization as large, calcified, and troubled as the US Army had become by the mid-1970s.

On the first morning of the course, the thirty men, organized into three training groups of ten, waited anxiously for class to begin. It seemed like hours before the classroom doors finally opened. When they did, the group Jack was in entered their classroom expecting to see a well-ordered arrangement of desks and chairs, an instructor's lectern, and a large screen at the front of the room for presentations.

Instead, they stepped into a bare room where twelve straight-backed chairs formed a closed circle, flanked by two easels standing like silent sentinels. One person muttered under his breath, "What the hell is this? What have I gotten myself into?" The others would share this sentiment in the coming days.

If the unconventional classroom arrangement was intended to start the students off on the wrong foot, it worked, and the inauspicious beginning continued to roll on. Starting time for class came and went. Minutes ticked by. The students' anxiety turned to anger as they waited for their absent instructors. When their patience had reached its limit, an army major walked into the room, wearing the same green uniform they all wore.

Everyone relaxed a bit. "Here finally," Jack thought, "is the instructor, a brother-in-arms." His name tag read "Cruz," and his presence provided a brief but welcome release from the mounting pressure. Yet something was still amiss—one chair remained vacant.

Moments later, a casually dressed man in his midthirties strolled in, his wire-rimmed glasses and reddish shoulder-length hair defying military norms. He introduced himself with a bright smile. "Good morning, everyone! I'm Gary Drexler. Welcome to the OE course! I'd like to know where your energies are this morning."

The officers were baffled. Energies? Jack's heart raced as he instinctively patted down his uniform, half expecting to discover something he'd forgotten to affix. "What does he mean by 'energies'?" Jack wondered, a creeping unease gnawing at him. "I hope what's happening starts making some sense."

Undeterred by the students' apparent confusion, Gary continued, "I'm so happy to be with you all this morning! This is the beginning of a great adventure we're going to have together! Will you each please introduce yourselves in turn? We'll begin to my left. Captain?"

Captain George Taylor, sitting directly to Gary's left, straightened in his chair. Jack thought, "Introduce ourselves? Our name tags and rank insignia are right here and clearly visible." But, beginning with Taylor, Jack and his classmates all complied.

"Good morning. I'm Captain George Taylor from the Eighty-Second Airborne Division."

Gary thanked Taylor and gestured for the next officer to continue. "Good morning. My name is Major Russ Smith. I'm here because I was told the skills I'll learn in this course will be good for my career."

Gary smiled warmly. "Excellent, Russ! I'm really glad to hear that!" The students noted his use of first names, the informality of which felt out of place in a military classroom.

Then came the introduction that shifted everything. The highest-ranking officer in the room, a lieutenant colonel, introduced himself without reference to his rank. "Good morning, everyone. My name is Norm House. Waiting to start was uncomfortable. I'm glad we've begun."

The group was stunned. A lieutenant colonel introducing himself by his first name was unheard of. Their confusion quickly turned to disbelief, but they did their best to mask their reactions and maintain their composure. A young captain sitting across from House, however, couldn't contain his emotions. Visibly seething, he looked at House and declared in a loud and breaking voice, "Sir, my name is Captain Bob Walker. I will never call you by your first name!"

And then, to the shock of everyone in the room, Walker began to sob—deep, uncontrollable sobs that left Jack and the other students frozen in place. Shocked, Jack thought, "This is the army. This can't be happening."

It wasn't that Jack or his new classmates were strangers to soldiers breaking down and crying. They'd seen it when people were wounded or had seen someone right next to them blown apart in a mortar attack. But this was different. They were in a classroom. Jack's mind raced, searching for a foothold in this unraveling scene.

Gary scanned the room, taking in the tension and raw emotions, knowing he had to act swiftly. Jack held his breath. "How can this civilian possibly handle what's happening? I hope to hell there's more to him than meets the eye." He didn't have to wait long for the answer. There was more—a lot more.

Turning to Colonel House, Gary asked: "Norm, I'm wondering how you're feeling right now?"

Norm responded, "I'm a bit embarrassed. I meant no offense in the way I introduced myself. I want Captain Walker and others to know they can address me in whatever way they're comfortable."

Gary nodded, gently encouraging Norm with a gesture to speak directly to Walker. "Captain Walker, I apologize. I meant no offense introducing myself as Norm. Please feel free to call me Colonel House as you wish."

The tension began to dissipate. Walker relaxed visibly, and Gary turned to him, addressing him by his first name. "Bob, what's going on with you right now?"

Walker, still emotional, explained, "I'm sorry. I've had a rough time the last few weeks. I had to leave my wife and new baby back in New Jersey. It's tough. I won't see them for four months."

Gary responded empathetically, "It sounds like leaving your family has been really hard on you. It's difficult to be away from loved ones, especially with a new baby. If you need to talk more, I'm here."

Walker thanked Gary and quickly turned to Colonel House. "Sir, I'd like to apologize to you for my outburst. I hope we can get to know one another better."

House, moved by Walker's vulnerability, crossed the circle and extended his hand. "No apology is needed, but I accept it. Thank you. I'd like us to get to know each other better too."

The two men shook hands, and in a spontaneous moment of emotion, Walker stood up and they hugged.

Jack watched as the group slowly began to process what had just happened. He felt a strange mix of relief and anxiety. "Is this what leadership in the new army is supposed to look like?" he wondered, feeling the weight of uncertainty settle in his gut. "If so, I'm not sure I'm ready for it. But maybe that's the point."

Nodding his head to Norm and Bob in acknowledgment, Gary then turned to the rest of the group and told them that he had three questions he wanted them to think about and be ready to discuss after they returned from a twenty-minute break: What happened in the last hour? Who was involved? and What was your reaction?

Gary already had a hunch about what he was going to hear and had formulated the outline of a plan to get ahead of it. During the break, he and his co-instructor, Major Ruben Cruz, fleshed out how they'd introduce the Content and Process Model and something they called the "power of how." This discussion would set the tone for everyone's journey through the OE course—and for some, the rest of their lives.

# 8 Understanding the Content and Process Model and the "Power of How"

> Sometimes when I write lyrics, there are images in them, usually on a quite simplistic level, like colors. But most often, music comes first, and then later, I sit down with visual people, and we chat about what we want to do. I don't look at myself as a visual artist. I make music.
>
> —Björk

Since the leadership concepts in this chapter came directly from Gary and Ruben, we decided to let them explain their ideas in their own words.

***US Army Organizational Effectiveness School. Same day.***

Gary Drexler was a gifted teacher. He understood that the morning's events offered a rare teachable moment—the brief window during or after an unexpected incident when people are most open and eager to learn.

Shaken by the confrontation between Captain Walker and Lieutenant Colonel House, the new students were keen to understand what had just happened. Gary seized the moment to introduce two fundamental leadership concepts: (1) what defines a group or team and (2) the Content and Process Model. He wrote five questions, labeled "Process Questions"—on one of the flip charts:

- What happened in the last hour?
- Who was involved?
- How did you react?
- What did you learn?
- What does any of this have to do with leadership?

He explained that process questions help people organize their thoughts about and reactions to complex events or experiences. He followed up by giving the class a specific assignment.

"I'd like each of you to think independently about what happened in the introductions this morning, and then answer each of these process questions for yourself. I'll get us back together in about ten minutes to discuss your thoughts."

When the discussion began, the students' initial responses were guarded, but as they grew more comfortable, their true feelings began to surface. Gary and Ruben noted these reactions, seeing them as additional insights into the group's dynamics. Here's a sampling of the points that were captured on the flip charts:

- "Half the time, I didn't know what was going on, and I was damned uncomfortable."
- "I didn't learn anything. What does what happened have to do with what I'll be doing if I continue and graduate from this course?"

- "I don't understand the relevance of what happened. Why are we beating it to death? I came here to learn about how to make the army more effective."
- "I learned that we need to establish some rules here."

Sensing the growing openness in the group, Gary dove directly into the two concepts he wanted to teach: what constitutes a group or team and the Content and Process Model.

## GROUPS, TEAMS, AND THE CONTENT AND PROCESS MODEL

"In the behavioral sciences," Gary began, "a group or team is when two or more people are together. And whenever they're together, two things are always happening simultaneously—content and process.

"Content," Gary continued, "is what's happening in the group—the tasks, conversations, or actions being carried out. Process, on the other hand, is how those things happen—the tone, body language, or emotions beneath the surface." He sketched the simple diagram shown in figure 8.1 on the flip chart, using a horizontal arrow to represent how both content and process unfold together over time.

Gary paused, reading the room. The students were alert, taking notes, and clearly intrigued. But he knew they needed more to be able to truly grasp the new ideas he was introducing. A quick glance at Ruben signaled it was time to move on to the next part of their plan.

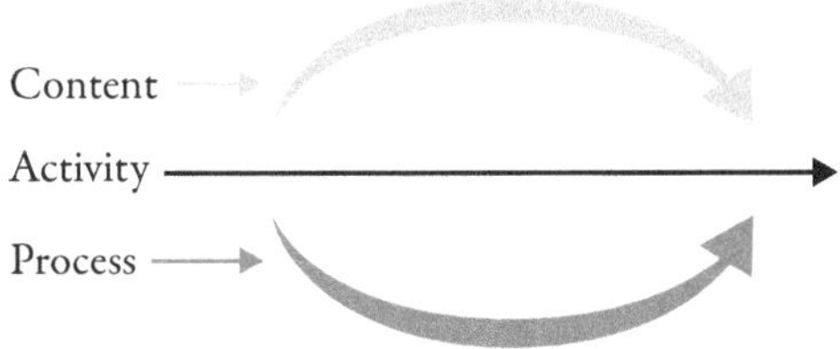


**FIGURE 8.1. THE RELATIONSHIP BETWEEN CONTENT AND PROCESS**

## WHERE WORDS FAIL, MUSIC SPEAKS

Ruben walked to the door, grabbed something, and brought it into the classroom. The room buzzed with curiosity. Smiling, Ruben began, "I see some of you eyeing my guitar case. There's no mystery. I've played since I was a teenager. This was a birthday present from my *abuela*—my grandmother. Are any of you wondering what a guitar has to do with what you're here to learn?"

He let the question hang for a moment and then said: "The short answer is, actually, quite a bit." With that he pulled out a beautiful twelve-string guitar. As he began to tune it, the room filled with bright, chime-like tones, captivating everyone. Anticipation grew. What would he play?

He didn't keep them waiting long. Playing the familiar chord progression from a song they all knew, "Leaving on a Jet Plane" by John Denver, he had their full attention. He began to sing the lyrics in his soft, melodic voice, telling the ageless tale of parting with loved ones, rekindling memories of students' own farewells.

Gary observed the group as Ruben played. "Leaving on a Jet Plane" wasn't just a song; it was a shared experience brought to life through music—a vivid demonstration of process in action, a moment where the "power of how" overwhelmed the "engine of what." He and Ruben would drive the point home.

The last notes from Ruben's twelve strings lingered in the air, carrying the weight of the moment. The students sat in quiet reflection, their thoughts drifting to memories and emotions that stirred something deeper than words. Some remained quiet, lost in their own thoughts. Others exchanged glances, an unspoken connection between them growing stronger.

With a nod from Gary, Ruben began to speak in a voice just above a whisper. "Lyrics are the words of a song that tells its story. It looked to me like you all connected with the story in this one." Heads nodded in affirmation, their expressions a mix of nostalgia and anticipation. They waited to hear more.

"Music is the other key element of a song. It's the arrangement of sounds that shapes and conveys mood and emotion. Together, music and lyrics engage both sides of your brain. Your left brain tracks the story, while your right brain feels and remembers the emotions the music stirs inside you."

Continuing, he asked, "What does any of this have to do with leadership? That's the right question—and one we're going to be asking a lot over the next sixteen weeks. In this case, two behavioral science concepts in leadership—content and process, or what and how, are the equivalents of the lyrics and music of a song.

"In other words, leading is not only about *what* you do but also *how* you do it." Turning a page of flip chart paper on a nearby easel, he revealed the graphic shown in figure 8.2 and proceed to walk the class through each of its elements.

Ruben began with the horizontal arrow, explaining that it represented any interaction or activity over time involving two or more people.

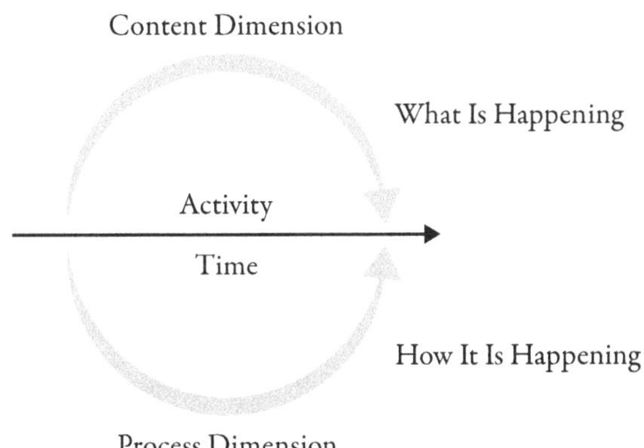


**FIGURE 8.2. THE CONTENT AND PROCESS MODEL**

Continuing, he said that the top half of the diagram, labeled the "Content Dimension" was the "what" of interactions or activities—a team conversation about a looming deadline, two colleagues enjoying a cup of coffee together, or Ruben playing a John Denver song."

Pointing to the bottom half, marked the "Process Dimension," he explained this was the "how" of interactions or activities, emphasizing that both content and process are present anytime two or more people are together.

"Both," he said, "play key roles in your daily life, at work and beyond. Let's take a closer look."

## WHAT CONTENT AND PROCESS LOOK LIKE

"We'll begin with content. You may not know this terminology, but you're very familiar with the idea. Content is nothing more than what you do, such as driving a car, counseling a soldier, or having a discussion with your spouse during dinner. Most of our lives, particularly our work lives, are almost exclusively focused on and dominated by the things we do—the content. But there's another important dimension called process.

"While content is what you do, process is how you do it. How we do the things we do is often overlooked in our push to get them done. Does this make sense to you?"

People indicated that it did, and Ruben continued. "The issue with ignoring process is that it has a big influence on how people react, engage, and perform. Here's an example I'll bet you understand.

"You can call someone an SOB, or son of a b—h in a certain way and get yourself into serious trouble—fast. Or you can say the exact same words another way, and you can get a laugh and a good-natured slap on the back. For the moment, what I want you to remember is that the how punches way above its weight in what psychologist William Schutz called the 'interpersonal world.'[1] Let me explain."

## A LOOK INTO THE INTERPERSONAL UNDERWORLD

"In leadership—like in music—a lot of what influences people happens beneath the surface, beyond what we've been taught to see or hear." Ruben flipped another sheet of flip chart paper to one with the image shown in figure 8.3 and said, "This graphic illustrates what I mean. Unsurprisingly, it's called the 'interpersonal iceberg.'[2]

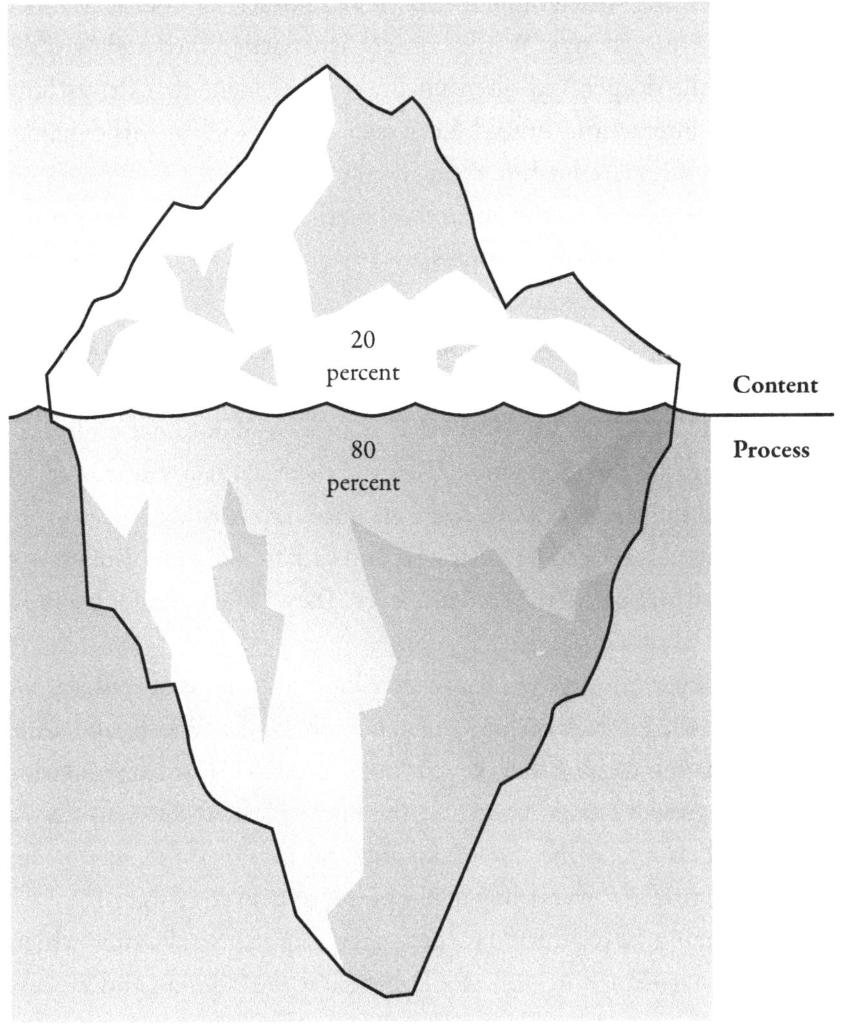


FIGURE 8.3. THE INTERPERSONAL ICEBERG

"Scientists say that only about 20 percent of an actual iceberg's total mass is visible to us, leaving approximately 80 percent hidden beneath the water's surface.[3] Content and process in the interpersonal world—which is where we interact with others—can easily be compared to an iceberg.

"We typically focus on what is happening—content. But like the tip of an iceberg, it's only about 20 percent of what's really going on. The other 80 percent, which often carries more significance, is process—the how of our interactions. While content is what's immediately visible, process is the deeper and often unconscious element that drives how events and interactions unfold. Let's take a closer look at this dynamic and how it affects leadership.

"Have you ever had the uneasy feeling that something is happening just outside of your consciousness, and even though you observed the event, it still feels like you missed something?"

Ruben guided the students' attention to the flip chart and bottom part of the iceberg drawing: "Here's the source of your uneasiness. This is where the how lives—and where it shapes the emotional undercurrents of every human interaction. The truth is that if you're not aware of process and the power of how, you have missed something."

He paused briefly to let what he'd said sink in. As it did, Ruben saw lights switch on behind the students' eyes. They'd made the connection. It was time to sum up.

"For the last hour, we've taken a close look at the ideas of content and process and their impact on human interaction. Understanding and using this information is going to be key in your success as OE officers and your continued growth toward becoming the kind of leaders the army needs. Gary and I, as well as the rest of the staff and faculty at this school, are committed to doing everything in our power to help you succeed.

"It's been a heavy-duty day. Let's take a quick break, after which Gary will wrap things up with a look at the way the Content and Process Model shows up in the real world."

## CONTENT AND PROCESS IN THE REAL WORLD

When the break was over, Gary led an illuminating discussion about how content and process influences virtually everything in people's lives. He scribbled on a flip chart and explained that almost everyone finds themselves working or living in one of three basic interpersonal environments:

Type A: Content-centric settings
Type B: Process-centric settings
Type C: Settings balanced between content and process

He proceeded to sketch diagrams of these three situations and explain each of them in turn.

### Type A: Content-Centric Settings

"Content-centric settings are the most common ones we experience as adults. They feel natural to us because we're raised focusing on the *what*, such as doing chores or homework. When we enter adulthood, our focus typically shifts to completing tasks and meeting deadlines."

While pointing to a new chart depicted in figure 8.4, Gary said, "Notice that in content-centric settings, the what dominates and how

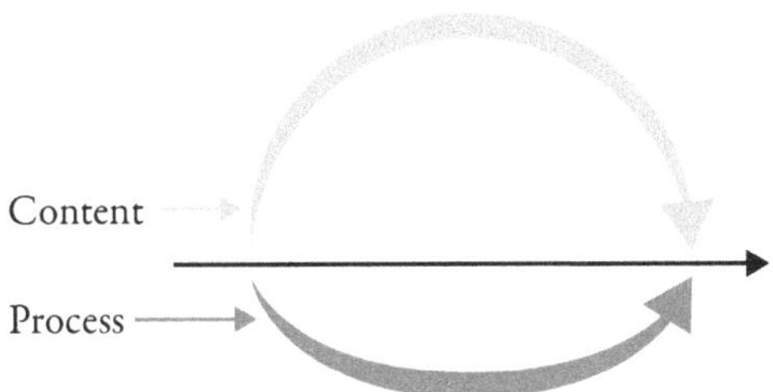


**FIGURE 8.4. TYPE A: CONTENT-CENTRIC SETTINGS**

barely exists. This content focus drives the short-term success of many content-centric organizations, such as the army. They're efficient, allow minimal distractions, and are places where things get done.

"My guess is that you expected a Type A classroom when you walked into this room earlier today. But it wasn't what you got." Gary flashed his Cheshire Cat grin, causing some of the group to snicker and others to wonder about his meaning.

"Be aware that while content-centric environments are efficient, they also have a downside. People exposed to a steady diet of content can and do eventually tend to feel undervalued, like they're just small, unimportant cogs in a big, insensitive wheel."

## Type B: Process-Centric Environments

"While Type A environments focus on the what, Type Bs use the opposite approach, placing more emphasis on *how*." Pointing to the graphic shown here in figure 8.5, Gary said, "Let's explore what happens when process takes center stage. Here's a Type B situation shown in the same kind of diagram you saw for Type A.

"Notice the relative sizes of content and process here. They're the reverse image of what you saw in the Type A diagram. Although rarer, Type B environments do exist. They're found in training groups, encounter groups, and group dynamics workshops.[4] In these settings, the focus is on how things are happening rather than what is

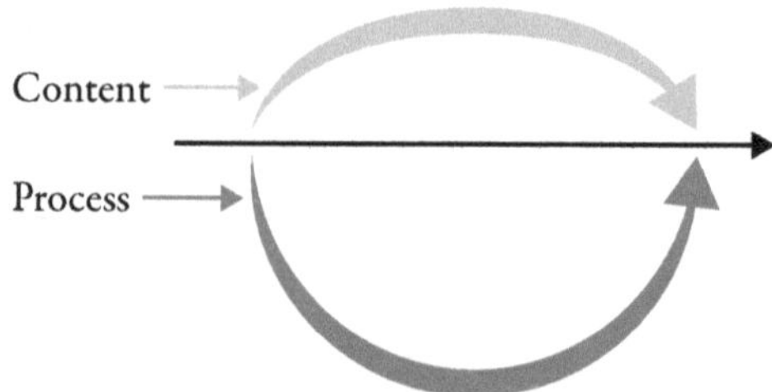


**FIGURE 8.5. TYPE B: PROCESS-CENTRIC SETTINGS**

happening. Emotions and feelings are on vivid display for everyone to see and hear.

"Just south of here at Big Sur, there's a place called the Esalen Institute.[5] It's a hub of the human potential movement, exploring human consciousness, personal growth, and alternative approaches to psychology, philosophy, and spirituality. If you asked me where you could learn more about Type B environments in your spare time, I'd tell you to check out Esalen. Short of that, you'll get plenty of experience right here. Our self-introduction session this morning was a good example of a process-centric environment."

Gary noted that grimaces appeared on more than a few faces, so he continued quickly. "No, no. Before you dismiss Type B environments entirely, let me point out a few of their advantages.

"Because they put a premium on openness and transparency, Type B settings offer numerous opportunities for giving and receiving interpersonal feedback. People don't hold back, which means in these situations, you'll know pretty much where you stand with others all the time. Finally, Type Bs encourage self-disclosure and promote the use of effective listening skills.

"On the minus side, in these Type B settings, people can get tangled up in interpersonal relationships, which sometimes leads to hurt feelings and personal animosity. In extreme cases, people lose sight of the work they should be doing and productive output grinds to a halt."

## Type C: Balanced Settings

"Now that we've explored the extremes—content-centric Type A and process-centric Type B settings—let's turn to the ideal balance: the Type C setting." Showing the class the graphic depicted in figure 8.6, Gary continued his explanation. "In this diagram, you can see content and process are in harmony, offering you and the teams you're leading the best of both worlds.

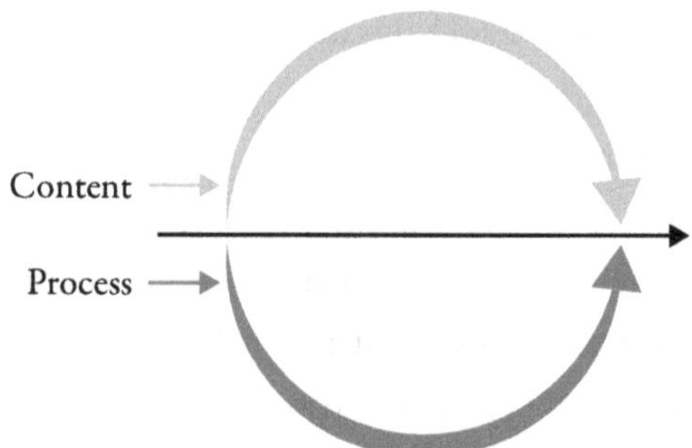


**FIGURE 8.6. TYPE C: BALANCED ENVIRONMENTS**

"Notice the relatively equal amounts of content and process, meaning there's a like amount of emphasis on what needs to be accomplished and also how it gets done. In addition to the variety Type C environments offer, they also give legitimacy to the process side of human interactions. Their openness and transparency encourages and supports team building, team development, and performance improvement. We'll be striving to create and maintain a Type C working and learning environment during our sixteen weeks together in this course.

"Finally, it's important for you to realize that in some organizations, particularly those characterized by command-and-control leadership approaches, Type C environments can carry the risk of being perceived as threats to the status quo. They can be interpreted as direct opposition to existing norms, values, and culture rather than well-meaning attempts to make improvements."

This last comment hit home and caused Jack, and he assumed others as well, to wonder once again, "What have I gotten myself into?"

## TRANSLATING CLASSROOM LESSONS INTO PRACTICAL APPLICATIONS

Gary began to wrap up. "We've spent most of the afternoon examining the concepts of content and process in the relative safety of a classroom setting. Luckily for you, you also got a taste of them during our self intros this morning, so you know they're not just eggheaded theories."

Pointing out the window, Gary said, "I assure you that content and process exist and are alive and well out there too. The difference is that beyond the confines of this room, the stakes are higher and the outcomes are more critical.

"I'm bringing this to your attention not to scare you but rather in the spirit of being straightforward with you. When you leave the OE course and get to your duty station, you're going to be swimming in a sea of content—the same one you were happily and ignorantly doing the back float in just a few days ago.

"What will be different when you leave here—and this is crucial for you to remember—is that you'll be seeing things that are related to process that few others around you will even have an inkling of, and it's going to be lonely for a while until you find your support system, which is a subject we'll return to later in the course."

## AN OVERNIGHT ASSIGNMENT

On that note—ever the teacher—Gary gave the group an overnight homework assignment.

"Imagine you've been assigned to lead a critical mission to disable an enemy missile site that's under construction that when completed will threaten friendly forces. You have thirty days to prepare your team.

"Based on what you've learned today about groups and the Content and Process Model, particularly the power of how, please be ready tomorrow morning to discuss what changes, if any, you'd make in the way you'd prepare your team for the mission from the way you'd have done it before today and why."

Ruben joined in, offering some questions for reflection: "First, reflect on your own experiences where a focus on content overshadowed process or vice versa. What happened? How did you react? What did you learn?

"Then, think about a time when a task or mission didn't go as planned. How much of that failure was due to a focus on the what rather than the how? How might things have been different if more attention had been paid to the process?

"Okay, it's been one hell of a day. Before we go, I'd like to go around the room and ask you each to sum up your reactions to the day in a single word. The only rule is, don't use a word that's already been used."

Although some students broke the rule and used more than one word, the exercise offered a perfect ending to a tumultuous day. Here's what the students had to say: "Surreal." "Mind-blowing." "Trying." "Gut-wrenching." "A university semester in a day." "Energizing." "Exhausting." "Eye-opening." "Every army leader needs to know this stuff." "Puzzling." "I'm lost." "Amazing." And "I can't wait to see what's next."

The lessons Gary and Ruben taught fifty years ago remain just as relevant today. No matter where or at what level you lead, your recognition of the power of how—or the lack of it—continues to shape every interaction you have and every activity in which you participate, bar none. This influence can create two dramatically different outcomes.

On one hand, many leaders are slow to evolve, still clinging to the outdated efficiency-driven model, where the focus is purely on content. This approach turns many workplaces into mind-numbing, soul-depleting environments, stifling human potential.

On the other hand, process-centric environments are increasingly becoming essential spaces for creativity, renewal, and growth. These settings span a surprisingly broad range of fields, including the following:

- *Food and beverage*—Farm-to-table restaurants emphasize the sourcing and quality of ingredients, focusing on process over simply turning tables to maximize profit.

- *Digital media*—Sites like Etsy, Substack, and GitHub celebrate craftsmanship, valuing the quality of creation and community engagement over volume.
- *Entertainment*—Audiences are increasingly drawn to authentic performances—both on the stage and on screen—that explore interpersonal dynamics.
- *Higher Education*—Stanford University's Graduate School of Business stands out in academia with its renowned course Organizational Behavior 374: Interpersonal Dynamics—colloquially known as "Touchy-Feely." This course focuses intensively on the how of human interaction, exploring its impact on relationship building and personal development. Celebrated for its practical approach to emotional intelligence and communication, Touchy-Feely remains one of Stanford's most sought-after offerings among students.

As we continue to navigate the complexities of the twenty-first century, it's crucial that we create opportunities and shape settings that offer balance and renewal—places that provide shelter from the relentless storm of modern life. In our workplaces, our homes, and, perhaps most significantly, our relationships with others, we must adopt and embrace a more humane, sustainable, and fulfilling way of living and working together.

The OE students in Gary and Ruben's class learned about content and process the hard way. It erupted all around them, delivering a sudden and unexpected shock. Fortunately, this occurred in a classroom environment dedicated to learning rather than in a real-world situation, giving them the chance to gain valuable insights with the help of two skilled instructors.

Unlike these students, you don't have to wait for a moment of crisis to learn. You can take a proactive approach to learning and mastering content and process. Taken together, they are, without exception, the foundation of the practice of effective leadership.

Understanding and applying the Content and Process Model may be one of the most valuable leadership skills you'll ever develop. It can help you improve every relationship in your life, at work and beyond. All it takes to become proficient is practice.

***US Army Organizational Effectiveness School. One day later.***

The next morning, the students came into class with their homework completed. They were ready to talk about how their understanding of content and process would affect their preparations for Gary's hypothetical mission to disable an enemy missile site.

When the discussion opened, not surprisingly, some of the students said they'd concentrate their team's preparation on concrete practice, rehearsals, map drills, and physical training. After all, up to now, this was what they'd been trained to do.

A few others talked about using a blended approach—mostly content-based steps, but with a little process added in, although they were unable to specify just what their process work would look like.

One of the most striking moments of the students' sixteen weeks of unforgettable experiences came when Wally Claussen, a major with two tours in Vietnam under his belt and a Silver Star Medal—the third highest US award for valor in combat—described how he would prepare his team after learning about content and process.

"Before yesterday," Wally began, "I'd have spent twenty-eight of my allotted thirty days of prep time on rehearsals, drills, and physical training. But after yesterday, I'd probably use three of those four weeks working with my team on process-related work, such as getting to know each other, sharing opinions about how to tackle different challenges, debating, arguing, watching old war movies, and taking our meals together."

The room fell silent. What Wally said gave everyone pause, foreshadowing the significant impact of what they were being exposed to. And they had only just started their second day.

Jack remembers Wally as a figure cut from the same cloth as Colonel Forrest, an officer he'd work for—or follow into combat—any day.

## EXTRAS: CHAPTERS 7 AND 8

### Chapters 7 and 8 Summary

- Jack and his classmates expected one thing and got its polar opposite on the first morning of their OE course. They'd never experienced anything like what happened.
- Luckily for them, they had two extremely caring and competent instructors who led them through their bewilderment, helped them make sense of what happened, and then began to connect the experience and their future roles in one of the most far-reaching culture change projects ever attempted.
- The students' learning began with a firsthand experience of the Content and Process Model: Content is *what* is happening. Process is *how* it's happening. Both content and process are always present together.
- Content is like mother's milk. You were raised on it. The trouble is that content alone doesn't adequately cover the whole of what's happening in human interaction. It's only the tip of the iceberg.
- Process—or how things happen—makes up the remainder. It can comprise up to 80 percent of any human activity. Whatever the numbers, process has a sizable influence. That fact alone is reason enough to study it carefully.
- The next time you have the feeling that you've missed something or have the sense that something has happened you just can't get a handle on, you can bet that you'll discover what you missed in the process dimension.
- The good news is that with a little effort and a lot of practice, you can learn how to see process right along with content as events

and interactions unfold. Better yet, you can become adept at actively managing it, which we'll discuss later in the book.

- Ask yourself these questions while you're observing process:
    - "What happened?"
    - "Who was involved?"
    - "How am I reacting? What am I feeling?"
    - "What's the lesson from this?"
- Working and living environments fall into three categories:
    - Type A: Content-centric settings, which focus more on what than how
    - Type B: Process-centric settings, which focus more on how than what
    - Type C: Settings balanced between content and process with similar amounts of focus on both what and how

## How to Use the Information in Chapters 7 and 8

We often get the question "How can I get better at seeing, understanding, and using the Content and Process Model?" Our answer is invariably that the best way to learn anything is to start small.

We define starting small with the Content and Process Model in an easy and enjoyable way—watching a classic movie or a contemporary megahit TV series.

We have two suggestions, beginning with the John Hughes's movie *The Breakfast Club.* Set in a suburban high school on a Saturday morning, the film tells the story of five student misfits who are serving an all-day disciplinary detention for violating various school rules during the week.

The interactions between this cast of characters is one of the best representations of human behavior in small groups ever captured on film—particularly at the process level.

In addition to its richness in opportunities to observe human behavior in action, Hughes's film also contains vivid examples of the heavy-handed command-and-control model of leading, the reactions this kind of leadership elicits, and how the disengagement it breeds festers and grows.

Our second recommendation is to watch any episode of the multiple-Emmy-winning comedy-drama television series *The Bear* created by Christopher Storer for Hulu. *The Bear* tells the story of a Michelin-starred chef who returns to his hometown of Chicago to take over his family's chaotic hot-beef sandwich shop in River North after his brother's death by suicide.

Of particular note is episode 6 in season 3, "Napkins," which features a long and intimate conversation between the character Tina, who's looking for a job, and Michael, the owner of the sandwich shop. The scene showcases one of the most touchingly human bits of filmmaking we've ever seen.

Whether you watch *The Breakfast Club* or *The Bear* (or both), you'll see how a small group, not unlike your own team of colleagues at work, deals with and resolves frictions, strengthens relationships, and bonds to create a shelter from the storms of work and life. To help you get the hang of observing content and process, make frequent use of your TV remote. When something happens in a scene that captures your attention or causes your stomach to flutter, hit the pause button, then use Gary's process questions to help you analyze it:

- What happened?
- Who was involved?
- How did the protagonist react?
- What did the protagonist learn?
- What does any of this have to do with leadership?[6]

Verse 11, *Tao Te Ching*

Although the wheel has thirty spokes
its utility lies in the emptiness of the hub.
The jar is made by kneading clay,
but its usefulness consists in its capacity.
A room is made by cutting out windows
and doors through the walls, but the space
the walls contain measures the room's value.
In the same way matter is necessary to form,
but the value of reality lies in its immateriality.
(Or thus: a material body is necessary to existence,
but the value of a life is measured by its immaterial soul.)

## Final Thoughts

We've seen how invisible dynamics in every human interaction can tip the scales when you're leading others. A couple thousand years ago, Lao Tzu, the author of the *Tao Te Ching*, held forth on what he called *immateriality,* a fancy way of referring to the subtle, unseen forces that often govern human interaction and leadership.

Jack and his classmates were blindsided by them. Reeling from the one-two punch of the conflict between Norm and Bob and then realizing they'd been missing over half of what was happening around them was almost too much for them to handle.

The insights they gained and the skills they learned were mirrored in the similar journeys taken by over 1,800 men and women who graduated from the US Army's Organizational Effectiveness Center and School during its ten-year existence (1975–1985).

One of the most consequential ideas these leaders were exposed to was that they could use their newly acquired skilled leadership knowledge metaphorically to do one of the following:

- Give people fish so they can eat today.
- Teach people how to fish so they can eat for the rest of their lives.
- Teach people how to teach others to fish so no one will ever be hungry again.

As leaders in the twenty-first century, we must become "fishers of people," teaching them how to teach others how to lead. This is how we start changing the world, one leader, one team, and one organization at a time. You can make a difference. Are you ready? Will you take the next step in your journey and join us?

# 9 Wake-Up Call

Everything that irritates us about others can lead us to an understanding of ourselves.

—Carl Jung

*US Army Organizational Effectiveness School. The third week.*

After their chaotic first day, Jack and his classmates gradually settled into the cadence of being in school again. The pace was relentless. By Friday of their first week, they felt like a semester's worth of postgraduate education had been crammed into their heads in just a few days. Exhausted but still buoyed by the excitement of learning new skills, they pushed through.

In the third week, their small training group of ten was divided into pairs for an observation assignment and tasked with watching—process observing—a leadership development workshop for noncommissioned officers. The student observation teams were told to observe only and not engage. Jack didn't have a problem with that—at least, he thought he didn't.

Their first day of observation passed without incident for Jack and his partner, Captain John Capriccio, an amiable young officer from the Third Infantry Regiment (the Old Guard), known for its spit-and-polish soldiers who guard the Tomb of the Unknown Soldier in Arlington National Cemetery. Day two proved to be different.

About an hour into observing the workshop, Jack's jaw tightened. Across the room, a young sergeant was speaking—his voice sharp, dripping with what Jack read as pretentiousness. Jack's pulse began to race. The sergeant's brash tone and the condescending way he dismissed his peers grated on Jack like nails on a chalkboard.

"Who the hell does this guy think he is?" Jack thought.

Jack's fists clenched so hard his palms ached. It was like staring into a mirror, and the reflection was ugly.

"My God, that's me."

The realization hit him hard, a wave of shame rising in his chest. That's exactly how he'd treated people since he came back from Vietnam—pushing them around, acting like he had all the answers.

His muscles tensed. The room felt hot and too small. He could feel the urge rising in him to stand up and tell the sergeant to knock the shit off. But protocol held him in place, a thin leash on his growing anger.

Instead, he grabbed his clipboard and scribbled furiously. The pen felt like an anchor in his hand, keeping him tethered to the moment. His thoughts poured out in disjointed fragments, messy and raw. His hands shook as he wrote, paper fluttering to the floor, but he didn't care.

Across the room, John was watching him. Jack felt his eyes but ignored him, focusing on the frantic movement of his pen.

Later, during the end-of-day debriefing session, Jack and John sat across from Gary and Ruben. Jack was still wound tight. Gary watched him closely, worry etched on his face.

"Jack," Gary said gently, a note of concern in his voice. "Ruben and I noticed you were tense earlier. What was going on?"

Jack stared at the floor, heat rising in his chest again. He stood abruptly, then paced a few steps. He was still angry, just barely keeping a lid on it.

"There's no sugarcoating it!" Jack snapped. "Every time that asshole opened his mouth, I got angrier. His combativeness, his arrogance—it was like looking in a mirror. It's the way I've been since the war, and looking at him, I saw myself staring right back at me. It was ugly."

Gary nodded, staying quiet, holding space for him to continue.

Jack ran a hand through his short hair, exhaling sharply. He gripped the back of his chair, knuckles white, and his voice wavered as the unfiltered truth finally poured out. "I've been walking around like some kind of hero—'Jack Barrett, super soldier.' But the truth? The war sucked. I did my job. I came back. Others didn't. And I've been acting like that makes me special, like I deserve to treat people however the hell I want.

"That sergeant today—I couldn't stand him because he was the reflection of the way I've been acting: pushing people around, pretending like I know best. It's BS. When I was about to explode, I remembered what the two of you taught us—the process questions 'What happened? Who was involved? How did I react? What did I learn?' So I started writing to keep myself from doing something stupid."

Ruben nodded to Jack and turned to John: "John, you were watching Jack closely. What did you see? And do you have any feedback you'd like to give him?"

Facing Jack, John chimed in immediately, "I saw you tense up, partner, but I wasn't sure why or how I could help. I get it now. The guy rubbed me the wrong way too. I think he's the antithesis of the kind of leaders the army needs—a caricature, really.

"I thought you were going to go nuclear, but you held it together. Good job! It seemed to me that the writing helped. I'm proud of you. I hope when my moment comes, I can keep my cool as well as you did today."

John paused, then added quietly, "I didn't know you were carrying all that garbage. I'm glad you got it out."

Ruben leaned in slightly, his voice calm. "Thanks, John. Good feedback." Turning to Jack, he asked, "What did you figure out through all of this?"

Jack hesitated, his voice quieter now. "I realized what a hypocrite I've been. I've been talking about the war like it was something noble, wearing my combat experience like it's some kind of badge of honor. But deep down, I hated all of it. I hate what I let it do to me. And I hate how I've treated people since I got back. I've been blaming them for my behavior instead of owning it."

His voice cracked, eyes flicking downward. "Even my wife and kids . . . I've been impossible to live with. I've said things like 'If you want me to treat you differently, then treat me differently.'" He shook his head. "That was just code for 'Do things my way.' What kind of life is that . . . " His voice trailed off, the full weight of his own words sinking in.

The room was heavy with silence, Jack's words still hanging in the air.

Ruben spoke again, his expression soft but serious. "Those are tough realizations, Jack, but important ones. It sounds like you're starting to see yourself more clearly. That's good. Real change starts that way. Self-awareness isn't easy. It's a process. And yeah, you'll stumble along the way. That comes with the territory."

The weight of his confession settled over Jack like a heavy blanket and the tension in his shoulders eased just a little. "I've got a lot of amends to make," Jack said, "and a lot of changes to figure out." Jack gave a small nod, this first step feeling weightier than he'd imagined. But at least now, he knew he was finally moving forward.

# 10 Becoming More Self-Aware

> The more you know about yourself, the more clarity there is. Self-knowledge has no end—you don't ever achieve it or come to a conclusion. It is an endless river.
>
> —Jiddu Krishnamurti

*US Army Organizational Effectiveness School.*
*Following the process observation practicum.*

Jack's experience in the process observation practicum was a turning point. It forced him to confront a version of himself that he didn't like—a wake-up call that spurred the long-overdue reckoning he'd been avoiding since he returned from Vietnam.

Like many returning soldiers, Jack felt disoriented and disconnected from his former life. Reconnecting with family and friends was difficult, and establishing new relationships seemed even harder. His candid admissions during the debrief with Gary and Ruben highlighted the depth of his struggle and the insights he had gained.

Despite the discomfort of this rude awakening, Jack considered himself fortunate. He had been given a gift—a new perspective on himself coupled with the confidence to change his behavior. He appreciated having access to mentors like Gary and Ruben, whose experience and wisdom were invaluable.

He was also aware that he needed a plan to continue make progress, but he hadn't yet distinguished between plans for immediate action and the longer-term strategy required for ongoing recovery and personal development.

## SHORT-TERM ACTIONS AND LONG-TERM PLANS

Like Jack, most of us want to tackle problems head-on, get them solved, and move forward. Although he didn't realize it, Jack had taken the first and most difficult step in formulating a short-term plan, which was to admit to himself that something was amiss. To his credit, he also knew he had fences to mend with others, and he actually began that humbling work.

Gary and Ruben coached him through the development of a longer-term strategy that would help guide his recovery from the trauma of war. When it was completed, Jack's long-term plan was anchored in three clear objectives: to shed the toxic postwar persona he had adopted, rediscover his authentic self, and reclaim the peace of mind he'd lost.

Almost everyone has hardships at some point in life—whether as the result of a difficult job, a failed relationship, a long illness, the loss of a loved one, or something else. If any of these have befallen you, or if you just want to make some improvements, developing a long-term plan is essential.

Formulating a plan might start with a few questions about what you hope to achieve: Who do you envision yourself becoming? What kind of person do you want to be? What kind of leader do you want to be? The changes you pursue don't need to be dramatic. Consider Jack's plan described above. It was simple: shed the toxic postwar persona he had adopted, rediscover his authentic self, and reclaim his peace of mind.

No matter your situation or circumstances, improving your self-awareness is a key part of the plan. You can wait for a crisis to force you into self-awareness, as it did with Jack, or you can take a more proactive approach.

To take the proactive route, you need to take two steps: (1) make the decision to move forward and (2) be willing "to let go of the side of the pool" and get out of your comfort zone. Whether you choose to take your chances or plan thoughtfully, this chapter will help you explore different perspectives of self-awareness and offer practical alternatives to simply rolling the self-awareness dice.

## A HISTORY OF SELF-AWARENESS

One of the most widely known references to self-awareness in modern culture is found in the science fiction cult classic film *The Matrix*. In a key scene, the protagonist, Neo, visits a woman known as the Oracle, who is said to be able to see the future. Neo is there to seek confirmation of his identity as "The One," whose presence she has foretold will signal the downfall of the Matrix, an evil software program that has enslaved humanity.

Instead of answering him directly, the Oracle points to a plaque above her kitchen door that reads *Temet Nosce*, Latin for "Know thyself," conveying to Neo that the answer can be found only within himself. While *The Matrix* is fiction, its message of self-awareness is timeless and deeply rooted in historical fact.

The phrase *Temet Nosce*, appears over the entryway to the Temple of Apollo at Delphi in Greece, which was established more than two millennia before the Wachowski sisters' movie. At this temple, the high priestess Pythia, also known as the Oracle of Delphi, dispensed her wisdom.[1]

The historical oracle was typically a woman over the age of fifty to whom the god Apollo granted future-seeing powers, making her a central figure who was consulted by leaders about many of the major happenings in the classical world. Her charge was to listen, advise, and provide guidance to those who sought her out.

Although the idea of knowing yourself and cultivating self-awareness goes back to ancient Greece, it might be even more important today. In the pages that follow, we'll explore three key questions to help you deepen your self-awareness: What is self-awareness? Why does it matter? And how can you become more self-aware?

## WHAT IS SELF-AWARENESS AND WHY DOES IT MATTER?

Self-awareness is often defined as the awareness of your own personality or individuality.[2] While accurate, this definition lacks practical every-day usefulness, particularly as it relates to leadership. To begin addressing this, let's explore self-awareness from several perspectives, starting with your internal understanding of yourself and then your perception of how you interact with others.

### Internal Self-Awareness

Your internal self-awareness is your private understanding of yourself, including your strengths, weaknesses, and limitations. The accuracy of your understanding depends on your ability to recognize and understand your own thoughts, feelings, beliefs, motivations, and actions.[3]

While internal self-awareness is crucial, it's only part of the picture. To be an effective leader, you also need external self-awareness—the ability to understand how others see you and how your actions impact them.

### External Self-Awareness

External self-awareness is often understood as the ability to recognize how others perceive you. However, this is only one part of a larger picture. A common misconception is that *others* refers only to people you know or work closely with, but that's not always the case.

A few years ago, Jack had a lively discussion with a retired army general about the role of external self-awareness in leadership. Jack maintained that it was about leaders understanding how they're perceived by the people they know.

The general listened carefully, and when Jack finished speaking, he asked, "So you're saying external self-awareness means understanding how people you know perceive you. Do I have that right?"

"Yes, that's it," Jack replied.

"Got it," the general continued. "Since you've had experience in both the army and the business world, I'm curious—what do you think about the old saying 'It's who you know' when it comes to career advancement?"

Without hesitation, Jack answered, "I think it's true. The more people you know, the wider your network, the better your chances for promotion."

"I used to think so too," the general admitted, "but since I was promoted to general, I've had some experiences that led me to see it differently."

Jack leaned forward, intrigued. "Please continue. I'm anxious to hear more."

The general continued. "Most people think career advancement is tied to external self-awareness through the idea of 'It's who you know'—specifically, your understanding of their perceptions of you. I've sat on many promotion boards that selected officers for promotion and for civilian education programs such as master's degrees and doctorates. Through those experiences, I was surprised to learn that who you know isn't the whole story.

"While external self-awareness requires understanding how people you know perceive you, that's not enough to ensure your selection for bigger jobs with more responsibility. To achieve that, you must understand it's also about who knows you—or knows of or about you. He had Jack's undivided attention.

"Put simply," the general summed up, "external self-awareness must also account for how people you don't know—and may never meet—perceive you and your actions."

It took Jack a moment to absorb this revelation. When he did, it challenged much of what he believed about external self-awareness, career advancement, and professional development.

Inspired by the general's insight, we decided to dig deeper into the concept of external self-awareness. What we found was eye-opening.

## WHO YOU KNOW AND WHO KNOWS YOU

In his 2007 book, *Personality and the Fate of Organizations*, Dr. Robert Hogan explores how personality can be used to "understand, evaluate, select, deselect, and train managers; to staff teams; and to understand organizations."[4]

Hogan's thesis is that an organization's future often hinges on the personality of a single individual, so great care must be taken when decisions are made about selecting people for key roles or offering professional development sponsorships.[5]

As a leader, you need to make sure your external self-awareness goes beyond the perceptions of those you interact with directly. It also has to include how people you may never meet—like a board chair, CEO, COO, or the heads of distant regional business units—perceive you based on your reputation. These individuals may decide what they're willing to do for you, offer you, or invest in you based solely on that impression.

Here are two key takeaways:

- *Cast a wider net*—When considering external self-awareness, remember that your reputation reaches beyond the people you know to others who don't know you personally and yet may still have formed impressions about your abilities and potential for advancement.
- *Build your reputation as a leader*—Become known for focusing on performance, caring for others, being willing to teach and learn, and leading as if people's lives and livelihoods depend on it. That's a reputation worth striving for.

## OTHER PERSPECTIVES ON SELF-AWARENESS

In his best-selling book *Emotional Intelligence*, psychologist Daniel Goleman defines self-awareness as knowing what you're doing while you're doing it—maintaining a "sense of ongoing attention" to your internal state.[6] Goleman's concept is like climbing a stepladder. At first, on the lower steps, you might not think too much about what you're doing—you've climbed ladders before. But as you climb higher, you start paying more attention to the potential risks and how your actions affect those around you. The higher you go, the more self-aware you become.

This brings us to two important points: First, the higher the personal stakes for you and those around you, the more you need to be self-aware. Second, self-awareness isn't a one-and-done kind of experience. Many assume that once they're self-aware, they'll stay that way, but that's not the way it works. You may be highly aware in one situation and completely oblivious in another.

As you saw in chapters 1 and 3, our protagonist, Jack Barrett, appeared to be fairly aware of himself during his wartime service. After his return home, however, you've also seen that he'd lost something during the transition from war to normal, everyday life. This kind of fluctuation is common; you can be highly self-aware when helping a colleague with a personal issue but completely insensitive when dealing with a similar problem of your own.

You're not alone. Research by organizational psychologist Tasha Eurich supports this. In a large-scale study, Eurich discovered that while most people believe they're self-aware, fewer than 20 percent actually are.[7] This gap between belief and reality highlights the difficulty of truly knowing oneself. It's like most other things worth knowing or doing: you have to work at it.

## SELF-AWARENESS FROM A BUSINESS PERSPECTIVE

During our research into self-awareness, we found another reason why knowing yourself is important, particularly if you work in any kind of for-profit business. Between 2010 and 2013, the Korn Ferry Institute conducted a study that found companies with a higher percentage of self-aware employees outperformed those with lower percentages.[8] When you think about it, this finding makes sense: self-aware employees, particularly those in customer-facing roles, are better equipped to build strong relationships, communicate more effectively, and adjust their behavior to suit different situations—all characteristics that contribute to business success.

## SOME TIPS ON BECOMING MORE SELF-AWARE

Having completed a brief survey of what self-awareness is and why it's important, let's turn to the question of how you can improve your own. We'll also offer a few tips on how to do so.

As we've mentioned before, we're big supporters of starting small and going slow so you can go fast later on. If you were training to run a marathon, you probably wouldn't try the full 26.2 miles on your first outing. You'd likely start out on runs of a mile or two and work your way up. You'd put in a lot of gym time and maybe start eating healthier. This same approach of starting small, going slow, and taking one step at a time will also serve you well as you're learning and helping others learn how to be more self-aware.

For example, it's easy to start small by regularly reflecting on your own behavior, asking for feedback from trusted colleagues, or engaging in mindful practices. We often advise people to couple these practices with one of our favorite structured self-awareness exercises, "Have To/Choose To," or HT/CT for short.[9] You can do this activity either alone or with another person you trust. HT/CT is easy and nonthreatening, and when done seriously, it hardly ever fails to produce insights into yourself that will surprise you. We've included detailed instructions for doing HT/CT in appendix B.

## EXTRAS: CHAPTERS 9 AND 10

### Chapters 9 and 10 Summary

- You need to have congruence between who you are and the work you do. The so-called wisdom that you should separate who you are and the work you do isn't true at all.
- Self-awareness is a springboard to getting better at being you. It's encapsulated in the timeless wisdom of the dictum "Know thyself."
- Self-awareness is being aware of your individuality in the context of your relationships and surroundings. It can be likened to climbing a stepladder:
  - On the lower steps, you're aware of what you're doing in the moment.

  - A few steps up, you become aware of the thinking behind your behavior.
  - Still higher, you're able to think about your thinking, what's called *metacognition,* and you become aware of the effect of your behavior on others. You're able to step outside of yourself and observe what's happening around you while you're knee-deep in action.
- Self-awareness is important from a personal perspective because it functions like an internal, onboard feedback mechanism.
- External self-awareness is the ability to understand how others perceive you, but it extends beyond those you know or work with directly. It encompasses the impressions held by individuals you may never meet, such as a board chair, CEO, COO, or leaders of remote business units. These perceptions, shaped by your reputation, can influence critical decisions about what opportunities, resources, or investments they are willing to offer you.
- Self-awareness is important from a business perspective because it's been proven that share prices for public companies with a higher percentage of employees who are self-aware outperformed those with a lower percentage.
- Self-awareness isn't a one-time event. You also can't assume that if you're aware of yourself in one situation, you will be in others.
- It's wise to do periodic self-awareness gut checks by asking yourself the following questions:
  - "What am I doing?"
  - "What am I thinking?"
  - "What thoughts led to my behavior and actions?"
  - "What impact is my behavior having on others and on me?"
- Our experience suggests that the explanation for the wide gap between belief and reality is related to fear. It can be frightening to learn about yourself. Seen and handled positively, it can be an exciting lifelong journey of self-discovery.

- We encourage you to work to become more self-aware. By doing so, you can make the best use of the rare privilege you have to make a unique contribution to your team's growth and development.
- Our best advice about how to become more aware of yourself is to start small and start slow. Remember, self-awareness is a process, not an event.

## How to Use the Information in Chapters 9 and 10

Our number-one suggestion is that you work your way through the "Have-To/Choose-To" (HT/CT) activity. This valuable tool can help you and your colleagues gain a deeper understanding of the dynamics of freedom of choice and personal agency.

According to the American Psychological Association, agency is "the state of being active, usually in the service of a goal, or of having the power and capability to produce an effect or exert influence."[10]

Encouraging personal agency is a fundamentally central but often-overlooked aspect of actual leadership. We will continue to raise the subject throughout this book.

You can improve your self-knowledge through numerous actions. Here's a short list of starters:

- Ask others for feedback. You'll be surprised at what they know about you that you don't know.
- Enroll in a personal development workshop led by experienced professionals. Don't waste your time with amateurs.
- Find and work with a psychologist who specializes in validated 360-degree feedback instrumentation, inventories, and other such diagnostic tools.
- Read lots and often—books, articles, blog posts, and anything and everything you can get your hands on that's relevant.[11]

- Let go of the side of the pool. Do things that take you out of your comfort zone. Use the process questions in chapter 8 to help figure out what you learned.

The ways to start becoming more aware of yourself are limited only by your imagination. Have some fun with it. Self-awareness needn't be something to dread, particularly if you're on an exciting journey of lifelong discovery. To quote the Buddha, "One may conquer a thousand men a thousand times in battle, but having conquered one's own self, one would surely be supreme in battle."[12]

Verse 28, *Tao Te Ching*

He who knows his manhood,
understands his womanhood,
becomes useful like the valleys of the earth.
Being like the valleys of the earth,
eternal vitality will not depart from him,
he will come again to the nature of a little child.
He who knows his innocence and recognizes
his sin becomes the world's model.
Being a world's model,
infinite vitality will not fail.

. . . . . . . . . . . .

Radiating simplicity, he will make men
vessels of usefulness. The wise man then
will the employ them as officials and chiefs.
A great administration of such will harm no one.

## Final Thoughts

Before we dive further into the rest of the book or explore any more of Jack's evolution as a leader, we need to briefly rewind to the late 1960s—a period marked by stark contrasts that laid bare humanity's perennial struggle between its more noble aspirations and its most loathsome instincts.

Positive developments during that time included the moon landing of Apollo 11, advances in civil rights, and the first Strategic Arms Limitation Talks (SALT), during which negotiators from the Soviet Union and the United States met with the aim of curbing the proliferation of weapons of mass destruction.

On the other side of the coin, however, grim events also occurred. Martin Luther King Jr. and Senator Robert F. Kennedy were assassinated. The Vietnam War continued to escalate, and the Soviet Union invaded Czechoslovakia. In other words, just like today, people had reasons to be wary and reasons to be hopeful.

Against this historical backdrop, our friend Jack Barrett had neither the time nor the energy to be either wary or hopeful. He was busy trying to navigate his own personal struggles, which included graduating from university, entering active military service as an army second lieutenant, and getting on with living his life. The late 1960s were a hectic time for Jack. He earned a bachelor of science degree and completed basic officer training and the army's airborne (parachutist) school where he learned how to jump out of—as they say—"perfectly good airplanes."

Reflecting on those accomplishments, Jack decided they were easy compared to where he then found himself. He was in the third, final, and most difficult phase of the army's Ranger training course, running on empty and needing a break that wasn't anywhere in sight.

In chapter 11, we join Jack in the treacherous swamps and sloughs of the Yellow River in Florida's Panhandle, waist-deep among alligators and water moccasins. In these unforgiving conditions, Jack learned a critical leadership lesson that didn't fully crystallize for him until decades later. Actual leadership has little to do with heroic gestures of profound significance. Instead, it revolves around a small collection of simple, everyday behaviors, similar to those you read about in chapters 2, 4, and 6 that related to the interactions between people who work together.

As we wade our way through the swamps of the Yellow River and the rigors of Ranger School with Jack, we invite you to reflect on the figurative swamps in your life and how your leadership behavior shapes your interactions with others. Then, ask yourself, "What lessons will I take from Jack's story?"

# 11 Dig In

The great enemy of communication,
we find, is the illusion of it.
—William H. Whyte

***The Yellow River, Florida Panhandle. December 1969.***

The Advent season, which begins on the fourth Sunday before Christmas, is celebrated by millions around the world in anticipation of the birth of Jesus of Nazareth. The word *Advent* comes from the Latin word *adventus,* meaning "coming" or "arrival." But in early December 1969, Second Lieutenant Jack Barrett wasn't anticipating any joyful arrival. He was simply waiting for his suffering to end.

Jack's misery, along with that of his sixty fellow Ranger candidates, was owing to the fact that they were in the final, grueling phase—the Florida, or Swamp, Phase—of the US Army's nine-week Ranger course. They were all that remained of a cohort of over a hundred and twenty soldiers who, in October, had begun what many believe to be the toughest leadership training course in the world.[1]

The Florida Phase of Ranger School contrasted sharply with the sun-drenched beachscapes depicted in travel poster imagery of the so-called Sunshine State. For Ranger candidates, Florida was an abiding ordeal of endurance where they were perpetually cold, wet, hungry, and exhausted. Wading waist-deep through menacing swamps day and night, not knowing what creatures lay in wait for them along the banks or under the water beside them, they soldiered on.

It was in this setting that Jack was assigned to be a member of a reconnaissance team whose mission it was to surveil a suspected enemy base camp—observe but not engage them—and report their observations to higher headquarters.

A reconnaissance (or recon) patrol is a small group of soldiers sent out to gather information about an enemy's position or the terrain features around it. Information gathered by recon patrols is typically used to help plan and conduct further military operations that reduce the risks to friendly forces.

Recon patrols are conducted with the utmost stealth and secrecy. Their success depends on the skill, training, and discipline of the soldiers involved, as well as their ability to use surveillance equipment, navigate challenging environments, and communicate effectively without compromising their own position.

Strangely enough, the recon training patrol Jack participated in during Ranger School was similar to the actual mission Jack and his team were assigned in Vietnam (chapter 3).

The suspected enemy base camp Jack's team was ordered to reconnoiter, role-played here by other soldiers, lay about twenty-five kilometers from where his team was located. Their orders were to proceed on foot at night so as to be in position to observe the enemy at first light the next morning. The prescribed route of the march to the enemy base was straight through what maps indicated was an "impenetrable swamp." The team's further orders were to rendezvous with friendly partisans at a designated set of map coordinates not later than twelve hours following the completion of their reconnaissance.

Eight hours into the swamp, cold and wet, the team eventually found some relatively solid ground and a welcome respite from the water and whatever creatures lurked around and beneath its murky surface. Happy to be momentarily drier, they sloshed along for about an hour when they were suddenly halted.

Rangers were trained to take up prescribed defensive postures for such occurrences. They fell to kneeling positions, weapons at the ready, and watched and listened intently. Fifteen minutes passed. Nothing happened. The halt turned into half an hour. Still no word came down from the team leader about what was going on.

Everyone continued to watch and wait. At the one-hour mark, whispers were passed from one team member to the next: "Dig in." No explanation was offered. The Rangers were incredulous, and by now, more than a few were "as pissed off as a Russian bear," as soldiers liked to say.

Around Jack, a handful of people broke out their entrenching tools, foldable minishovels they all carried, and began hacking away at the soggy ground. Shallow holes filled with water almost instantly. Many others, including Jack, hesitated. The dig-in command made no sense. They came within a hair's breadth of refusing it, a decision that could have spelled mission failure—and their immediate expulsion from the course.

Watching their teammates work their butts off trying to dig foxholes, Jack and the others finally relented—but only half-heartedly by going through the motions. As he scraped at the earth, a stream of thoughts flashed through Jack's mind: "Why are we halted? How are we supposed to dig in through these roots and vines and soupy ground? What's the point of all this? What's the team leader thinking? This is complete BS! We need to know what we're doing for sure, but that's not enough. A word or two about why would make all the difference. I swear, when I'm through with all this playing soldier, and I'm leading troops for real, I'll tell them what's going on. I'll never just order them to 'dig in.'"

Jack's frustration in the swamp was a pivotal leadership experience. He saw and felt firsthand what everyday soldiers went through, and it wasn't pretty. It led to one of his most significant takeaways from Ranger School—that relevant information must be timely, delivered respectfully, and communicated in a way that fosters understanding, acceptance, and learning. Simply issuing instructions may pass enough information to get the immediate job done, but it seldom does anything to help either you or its recipients understand, grow, and develop proficiency.

Jack's experience in Ranger School also taught him a thing or two about the limits of human endurance, which is encapsulated here in a sanitized version of an old Ranger truism: "You can walk through the woods for a long time with your finger stuck in a bear's ear if you have to."

The difficulty for Jack personally was never the woods or the walking, the swamps or the wading—or even the bears. It was, and still is, communicating the right information in the right way at the right time to get the job done.

# 12 Turning Information into Communication

> Take two popular words today, "information" and "communication." They are often used interchangeably, but they signify quite different things. Information is giving out; communication is getting through.
>
> —Sydney J. Harris

You've likely experienced times in your life when you feel like you're right there alongside Jack, up to your armpits in alligators, uncertain of your next steps, and trying to navigate your way through your own personal version of a swamp.

In these moments, knowing the distinction between information and communication and then being proficient in turning the former into the latter can mean the difference between sinking deeper into the muck or striding out of it with confidence.

This chapter offers practical steps to transform information into communication that connects with others and inspires them to action. To set the stage, let's travel to the windswept dunes of Kitty Hawk, North Carolina, where two brothers turned raw data into a history-changing breakthrough.

## KITTY HAWK, NORTH CAROLINA, DECEMBER 1903

Orville and Wilbur Wright, bicycle mechanics from Ohio, stood on the windswept dunes of Kitty Hawk beside the *Wright Flyer*—a delicate structure of wood, wire, and canvas—poised for its maiden flight. Years of relentless tinkering, studying wind currents, and exchanging ideas had led to this moment. As Orville climbed aboard, Wilbur called out last-minute adjustments above the roar of the wind. Their achievement wasn't just a breakthrough in aviation. It was a triumph of communication: transforming raw data on lift and drag into a shared vision that, for twelve historic seconds, carried the *Flyer* into the air.[1]

The Wright brothers succeeded because they communicated clearly, aligned their efforts, and acted as one. Leadership requires the same capacity: to transform information into communication that fosters clarity, connection, and coordinated action. This chapter invites you to explore that distinction—between information and communication—and why it matters so much to leadership.

## ABOUT INFORMATION AND COMMUNICATION

Let's dive directly into the process of turning information into communication, beginning with a closer look at what each of these words actually means.

### Information

*Information* is defined as the "representation of knowledge such as facts, data, opinions, or instructions in any form."[2] Its nature, as Sydney J. Harris noted in this chapter's epigraph, is to be given out to others, which creates awareness—whether about a new policy, a change in a work process, or the launch of a new product. As powerful as that cognizance may be, this aspect is only a part of a much bigger picture.

Information comprises the literal building blocks of life, as encoded in the DNA of every living organism. It determines that an oak tree is an oak tree and not an evergreen and also why there's no one else anywhere just like you.

Some scientists even argue that information organizes all matter and energy, explaining that energy shows up in various forms, such as light waves, thermal energy, and sound.[3] Closer to home, think about how you arrange the finite letters of your alphabet to form words and convey thoughts. Depending on how you organize them, their meanings can be as different as day and night—literally.

We use information every day to help structure our ideas and actions, but alone, it's insufficient for leading others. It can't explain the big picture, break difficult news emphatically, or win your team's buy-in. It won't create the kind of sustained dedication that's one of the hallmarks of high-performance teams. For that, you need information's big and more clever sister, communication.

## Communication

Effective communication is more than simply sharing information or giving instructions; it's the exchange of meaning between people through a common system of symbols. Virtually everyone wants—and often needs—to understand the reasons behind tasks they're expected to perform. A basic understanding of human nature supports the fundamental truth that when we grasp why we are doing something, we tend to perform better. Best-selling author Simon Sinek wrote an entire book on the subject, telling his readers to always *Start with Why*.

Jack and his Ranger School classmates' performance on their recon patrol would likely have been better in the swamp if they'd understood more about why they'd been ordered to "dig in." As it was, they learned an important leadership lesson from a negative example. Jack in particular promised himself that, going forward, he would always do his best to try to explain the reason behind what he asked people to do—even if it was only a word or two.

Later, he discovered that inviting questions and providing clear explanations built goodwill and improved team performance. Delivering the right information at the right moment—and in the right way—almost always paid off.

What worked for Jack in his day is even more critical for you in today's fast-paced, globally connected world. Consider the contemporary story of how CEO Larry Culp is actively and positively transforming General Electric Company's culture, as reported in *Bloomberg*.[4]

Culp and his team rely on direct, face-to-face communication to guide GE's workforce toward excellence. A key practice is the "gemba walk," rooted in the Toyota Production System's "genchi genbutsu" principle, meaning "go and see for yourself."[5] By observing processes firsthand, leaders make informed decisions, a practice revitalized at GE under Culp's leadership.

Imagine if the leader of Jack's patrol in the swamp had taken a similar approach. By seeing the near impossibility of digging foxholes in waterlogged ground, he might have reconsidered his order or at least provided some rationale to clear up his team's confusion. Had he done so, he would have unknowingly been on the path of turning information into communication.

## TURNING INFORMATION INTO COMMUNICATION

You've seen Jack stuck—both literally and figuratively—waist-deep in the muck of an unforgiving swamp, where every movement only seemed to pull him deeper. Does this feel familiar? As a leader today, you may easily feel like you're navigating a maze of interconnected problems, with the way forward being anything but clear, making the challenge of communicating to your team even more daunting.

We created the SHARE (signal, highlight, align, rally, execute) Model for times when the traditional practice of giving out information won't suffice. SHARE is a five-step process that turns information into communication. Picture it as a path, with each step moving you closer to your goal. Skip steps, and your message falters; follow them, and you create trust, engagement, and results. Let's explore SHARE using a modern-day leadership scenario that could happen in your organization.

## A MANAGER'S CHALLENGE

Makayla, a manager, is about to launch a new customer relationship management (CRM) system to improve sales tracking. Her team is skeptical, wary of another tech overhaul. She uses SHARE to guide them step by step from awareness to action.

### Step 1: Signal—Announce the Change Clearly

Makayla signals the change to ensure awareness. She sends an email outlining the CRM's launch date and purpose. Then, she has a team meeting to preview its impact. She keeps it simple, inviting questions to spark interest.

Take these steps to successfully signal:

- Be transparent by sharing key details (e.g., "The CRM launches next month to track clients better.")
- Choose appropriate communication channels based on your team's preferences—such as emails, meetings, or visuals.
- Pique curiosity by highlighting why the change matters.

Signaling ensures everyone knows what's coming.

## Step 2: Highlight—Explain the Reasons for the Change Transparently

Makayla highlights the reasons for the new CRM system, connecting it to team goals. She shares a story of a lost sale due to poor tracking and data showing a 25 percent efficiency gain in a pilot, then invites questions to clarify the "why."

Take these steps to effectively highlight:

- Link changes or tasks to team goals. Show how the change drives success (e.g., "This boosts sales and cuts busywork.").
- Use stories and data to help make the rationale tangible.
- Encourage dialogue by leading question-and-answer sessions to promote deeper understanding.

Highlighting builds a clear case for your team.

## Step 3: Align—Foster Buy-In

To gain her team's buy-in, Makayla opens a dialogue. In small group chats, she addresses concerns about the CRM's learning curve with a demo and emphasizes ways it will save time. She asks each member to share their thoughts, confirming their buy-in.

Take these steps to successfully align everyone:

- Listen actively to make sure you understand people's concerns. Address doubts with empathy (e.g., "I hear your worries about training. You have my word, we'll provide support.").
- Emphasize benefits that accompany the change. Highlight positives for the team, such as easier workflows.
- Verify understanding and buy-in by asking for feedback.

Aligning creates support.

## Step 4: Rally—Secure Commitment to Support

In this step, Makayla rallies the team by organizing them for success. She assigns team leads to champion CRM adoption and praises their skills. She shares a pilot team's early success, which boosts confidence and commitment.

Take these steps to effectively rally your people:

- Set people up for success by assigning clear roles (e.g., "You'll be the team's CRM trainer.").
- Build team unity by emphasizing shared purpose.
- Share early successes to fuel forward progress and momentum.

Rallying turns buy-in into dedication.

## Step 5: Execute—Drive Action to Implement

Just as she is responsible for creating the conditions within which her team can perform, Makayla is also on the hook to ensure action. She provides hands-on CRM training, tracks a 20 percent uptick in client follow-ups, and adjusts the team's goals based on feedback. She celebrates progress with team recognition, which keeps their momentum headed in the right direction.

Support execution by taking these steps:

- Provide training and other resources as needed.
- Track results by measuring progress and sharing updates.
- Adapt and celebrate by making small refinements as you go and rewarding achievements.

Executing brings the shared goals to life.

Picture the SHARE Model as a staircase you and your team must climb, as shown in figure 12.1. Each step builds momentum, bringing you closer to success. Skip a step or take shortcuts, and your momentum falters. People want to be involved, understand, and contribute. As a leader, you need to create the conditions that make it possible for them to do so.

Table 12.1 shows a handy at-a-glance SHARE reference guide that describes each step.

## MASTERING THE USE OF INFORMATION AND COMMUNICATION

You've likely come across the saying "A goal without a plan is just a wish." With this in mind, you can easily convert the at-a-glance graphic in table 12.1 into a simple communication plan to help you accomplish your most important communication tasks.

Having a well-structured communication plan ensures that your critical messages consistently reach your audience. To support you in this effort, we've included notes on how to develop such a plan, along

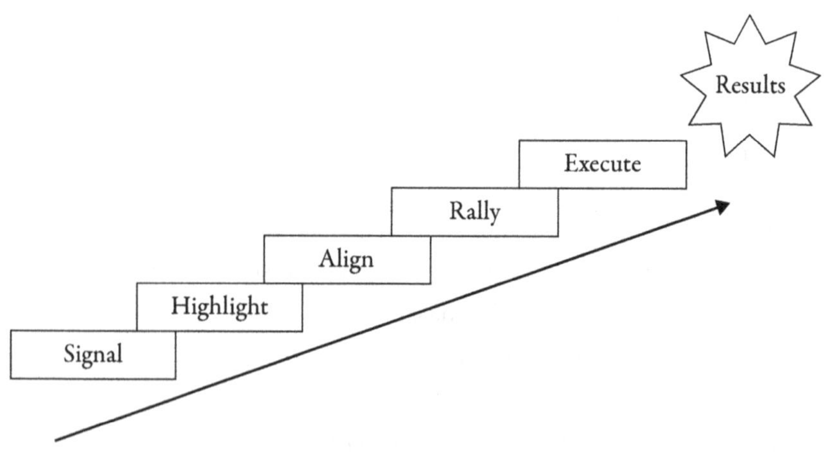


**FIGURE 12.1. THE SHARE PROCESS**

**TABLE 12.1. SHARE AT A GLANCE**

| Step | Description | Outcome |
|---|---|---|
| Signal | Announce the change | Consciousness |
| Highlight | Explain the reasons for the change | Comprehension |
| Align | Foster buy-in | Conviction |
| Rally | Secure active support | Commitment |
| Execute | Drive implementation | Contribution |

with a sample framework, in appendix C. These tools are designed to help you communicate clearly, effectively, and with purpose every time.

## QUESTIONS FOR REFLECTION

Take a moment to reflect on a time you introduced a new process to your team. Did your message resonate with them, or did confusion cloud their understanding? Did you achieve engagement, or did you get the sense that people just went through the motions? Thinking through these questions can show where SHARE might help turn challenges like this into opportunities.

Most people who learn about SHARE rate it as one of the most practical and useful pieces of skilled leadership knowledge they've ever learned. We encourage you to give it a try.

## EXTRAS: CHAPTERS 11 AND 12

### Chapters 11 and 12 Summary

- Information is the "representation of knowledge such as facts, data, opinions, or instructions in any form."

- Communication is the exchange of meaning between people through a common system of symbols.
- Informing is about getting the word out to people. Communicating is about getting it through to them.
- Effective communication is central to the process of leading.[6]
- Timely, relevant information that is delivered respectfully and communicated in a way that fosters understanding, acceptance, and learning enhances performance.
- Inviting questions and providing clear answers strengthens engagement and prevents dissatisfaction and worse.
- SHARE is an acronym for signal, highlight, align, rally, and execute, a simple but effective communication process.
- The signal and highlight steps of SHARE are primarily about the what, or the content, you wish to communicate. The align, rally, and execute steps are more closely related to the how, or process you use to communicate it.
- A communications plan is a framework to organize and use information in each step of the SHARE process to help you achieve your specific communication outcomes, and developing this type of plan ensures that the process of turning information into communication is never left to chance.

## How to Use the Information in Chapters 11 and 12

To stimulate your inner Wright brothers, we've created a list of information-and-communication-related questions for you to think about and answer as your time and spirit allow.

- When's the last time you personally visited the people who are creating in your team or organization to see their work for yourself?

- What's it like when you see your team's work in-person for yourself?
- On a scale of one (a little) to five (a lot), how much does seeing the operations for yourself help you make more informed decisions?
- How often do you engage your team in two-way, face-to-face discussions?
- How self-aware do you think you are about whether, as Harris puts it in the chapter epigraph, you're "getting through" to others instead of merely giving information out to them? What's your evidence?
- If asked, what do you think your colleagues and teammates would say about how you use information and communication?
- What specific steps might you take to make how you communicate more craft-like?
- What specific information could you turn into communication in your daily work that might make the difference in how your team performs?
- What part of the gap between your team's actual and potential performance do you think is related to how effectively you use information and communication?
- What, if anything, does any gap between your team's actual and potential performance have to do with your team's or your own lack of awareness and understanding of the Content and Process Model discussed in chapter 8?

Verse 15, *Tao Te Ching*

In olden times the ones who were
considered worthy to be called masters were
subtle, spiritual, profound, wise.
Their thoughts could not be easily understood.

Since they were hard to understand
I will try to make them clear.
They were cautious like men
wading a river in winter.
They were reluctant like men
who feared their neighbors.
They were reserved like guests
in the presence of their host.
They were elusive like ice
at the point of melting.
They were like unseasoned wood.
They were like a valley
between high mountains.
They were obscure like troubled waters.
(They were cautious because
they were conscious of the deeper
meanings of life and its possibilities.)

We can clarify troubled waters
by slowly quieting them.
We can bring the unconscious to life
by slowly moving them.
But he who has the secret of the Tao
does not desire for more.
Being content, he is able to mature
without desire to be newly fashioned.

## Final Thoughts

Congratulations and thanks for sticking with us through parts 1 and 2, setting the stage and laying the foundation for leading, respectively.

You've read about some of the most significant lessons of Jack's early leadership career: during his time in the war in Vietnam, at the army's Organizational Effectiveness (OE) school in California, and in the swamps of the Florida Panhandle.

Along the way, you've explored the core of actual versus illusory leadership, the three pillars of leadership: mindset, skilled knowledge, and personal sensibilities as encapsulated in the Leadership Actually Model.

You've examined many parts of this model—all of which are full of insights into ways you can make leadership your professional craft. You've seen the importance of self-awareness, learned about the Content and Process Model, and discovered how to transform information into communication your team can understand and act on.

And the best is yet to come. In the third and final part of *Leadership Actually*, we'll dive into the three most impactful skills of actually leading with craft: managing team process, fostering a team culture of shared learning, and co-creating with others.

As you look back on what you've already read and look forward to what's next, it's worth giving some thought to how you can apply any or all of it in your own work.

# PART 3

# Doing the Doing of Leading

In parts 1 and 2, we set the stage and laid the foundation to lead by doing the following:

- Examining the pillars of leadership—mindset, skilled knowledge, and personal sensibilities (chapters 1–4)
- Introducing the notion of leadership as a craft (chapters 5 and 6)
- Illuminating the distinctions between content and process (chapters 7 and 8)
- Highlighting the importance of self-awareness (chapters 9 and 10)
- Emphasizing the centrality of communication (chapters 11 and 12)

In part 3, we're going to shift gears, roll up our sleeves, and dive into doing the doing of leading, where we'll maintain our balance between lessons learned, key concepts, and practical application. We'll also begin weaving together and applying the concepts we've built so far, enabling the broader vision of *Leadership Actually* to start to take shape as we address managing team dynamics, teaching and learning together, and co-creating with others.

As we move ahead, you'll see how to combine and mix and match these elements and use them in ways that fit your particular leadership circumstances.

# 13 Paradigm Shift Revisited

In the midst of chaos, there is also opportunity.

—Sun Tzu

***The first morning of the OE course. 1976.***

You'll recall from chapter 7 how the unorthodox arrangement of the OE classroom—a barren circle of twelve chairs and two blank easels—fueled anxiety among the assembled officers. No desks, no lectern, no comforting symbols of military order. Just empty space that echoed the unspoken dread of what might come next.

The clock was no help. Minutes ticked by, well past the expected start time. No instructors had arrived. Uneasiness thickened, settling over the room like the fog in Monterey Bay.

The students weighed what was happening: it was either a series of inexplicable mistakes or, God forbid, a deliberate affront to their soldierly sense of punctuality and order. In truth, something much more profound was happening.

The events that played out that morning weren't just about a delayed beginning or an unconventional classroom setup. They were about process unfolding in the midst of orchestrated chaos, intentionally designed to provide the students a first taste of experiential learning. The events also served as a welcome to the paradigm shift that the next sixteen weeks would represent—for the students themselves, their families, and the army as a whole.

When Gary finally entered the room, casual and unruffled, his sunny demeanor was in sharp contrast to the brittle tension almost palpable in the classroom. "I'd like to know where your energies are this morning," he said with a wide, disarming smile.

The question was so baffling, so alien to the students' world of strict hierarchy, regimentation, and concrete objectives, that it threw the group into a state of utter confusion. They hadn't seen anything yet.

Lieutenant Colonel Norm House's self-introduction shattered the last fragile hope that this was just a rocky start that would soon give way to normalcy. House, the highest-ranking officer in the student group, had chosen—astoundingly—to introduce himself using his first name. "Good morning, everyone. My name is Norm House." Technically, it was his name. But the way he used it in that environment felt to Jack and others like someone had lobbed a hand grenade into the room, shattering the traditional military paradigm of top-down, rank-based authority the students were familiar with and expecting.

They didn't realize it at the time, but that moment offered a first glimpse into what would become one of the most powerful leadership skills they would ever acquire: managing team process. Over time, this know-how would come to shape their entire understanding of what real leadership looked like in practice. They would come to see how authority, influence, vulnerability, and emotion are always at play beneath the surface of every team—and, more importantly, how to manage these dynamics for the good of all.

But in that first hour, all they really understood was the visceral shock delivered to their psyches when Bob Walker reacted to Norm House's self-introduction. Sobs and tears broke free as he declared that he would *never* call a senior officer by his first name. The outburst upended everyone—everyone, that is, except Gary Drexler.

Gary's calm, empathetic response diffused the tension and brought the group back to an even keel even though the tremors continued.

Jack, for example, was still reeling. What did this incident and the way it was handled mean for him, the way he led, and the work he was destined to do when he graduated?

Neither he nor any of his classmates could grasp the full scope of what had happened or what it foreshadowed. As Gary began to introduce the Content and Process Model, Jack sensed he was standing at the threshold of something transformative—and terrifying.

# 14 Managing Team Process

It's not what happens. It's how you handle it.

—Jill Telford

In chapter 13, you saw an accomplished leader in action—one who could read the room and recognize that more was happening beneath the surface than the students' words and actions revealed.

Gary's understanding of the Content and Process Model enabled him to master one of the most crucial—and often overlooked—elements of skilled leadership knowledge: managing team process. In this case, Gary did the following:

- Tuned in to the group's emotions, such as anger, confusion, and discomfort
- Quickly and accurately assessed the stage of their group process
- Applied leadership behaviors proven to be effective at that stage

His goal was to guide the group toward a quieter, more reflective space so he could help them understand what had happened, not just between Bob Walker and Norm House but with all of them as vicarious observers.

On the surface, mastering these skills may sound like a daunting task. We know because that's how it felt to us when we were students. But take heart: this chapter will unpack these skills and provide you with the knowledge to apply them in your own team—whether you lead in a classroom, conference room, mailroom, locker room, or operating room. Together, we'll explore the following topics:

- What team process is and why managing it is critical for effective leadership
- The four stages of the 4-C (convening, challenging, cooperation, and collaboration) Team Process Model and how they show up in teams like yours
- Insights from the leadership vignettes featured in this book's odd-numbered chapters that illustrate the 4-C Model in action
- Quick-reference tools for each stage, inspired by Dr. Robert Mager's concept of "job aids" from his book *What Every Manager Should Know about Training*[1]
- A fast and easy way to ensure you always use the most effective leadership behaviors for each stage of team process

With this brief introduction, let's begin to explore the important and exciting world of managing team process. It's easily the most powerful and consequential of any piece of skilled leadership knowledge you're likely to come across.

## TEAM PROCESS AND WHY IT'S IMPORTANT

The term *team process* means the evolving and repeating patterns of interactions—or stages of team development—your team experiences as it works together over time. This concept is supported by decades of academic study and research, including Bruce Tuckman's stages of group development and Schutz's theory of interpersonal relations.[2]

Most team process models provide descriptions of the common stages teams go through. Few, however, describe how to use them in action. We will. But regardless of the model you use, the goal of managing team process is to make working together in your team smoother and more effective.

As one of our workshop participants once observed, "When you're managing team process, it's like applying WD-40 lubricant to your team's interactions—it reduces friction and helps people work together more smoothly." This comment perfectly captures the essence of this crucial leadership skill.

But there's more. Managing team process not only reduces friction; it also helps you create a safe environment for your team. When people know you're actively monitoring and guiding their interactions toward the successful accomplishment of goals, they feel safer to be more fully themselves, take risks, and engage more openly. Your ability to manage team process is a win for everyone.

Toward that end, we created the 4-C Team Process Model to help simplify what can often be seen as a complex undertaking requiring an advanced degree in psychology. The 4-C Model is a practical framework that focuses on how you can use it in your team regardless of the stage of development. Let's take a look at how this works.

## AN OVERVIEW OF THE 4-C TEAM PROCESS MODEL

Imagine managing team processes as if you were driving a car with a manual transmission. Doing so requires knowing the gearshift patterns, recognizing when to change gears, and mastering these techniques through practice. The same principles apply to managing team process effectively.

The 4-C Team Process Model mirrors the gearshift pattern. Each of the four gears corresponds to a distinct stage of team process: convening, challenging, cooperating, and collaborating, as shown in figure 14.1.

Just as different driving situations—starting out, building momentum, gaining speed, or cruising—have their own ideal gear, each stage of the 4-C Model works best when it's aligned with specific leadership approaches that have been proven to be most effective in each stage. More on this shortly.

Becoming proficient at managing team process is like mastering a manual transmission: it requires both a solid understanding of each stage and consistent, hands-on practice.

The goal of managing team process is simple but significant: ensure your team works together smoothly to achieve its objectives. To lead well, you must be able to observe team dynamics, recognize the subtle signals that indicate a team's developmental stage, and identify that stage with clarity. This dual ability—intuitive recognition combined with thoughtful identification—is what enables you to respond with intention rather than impulse.

Much like as an experienced driver shifts gears to keep the car moving smoothly, a skilled leader guides the team through transitions between stages with similar ease. Progress often means moving forward, but sometimes it requires downshifting to adjust to changing conditions. Unlike a car, however, team process has no true reverse gear.

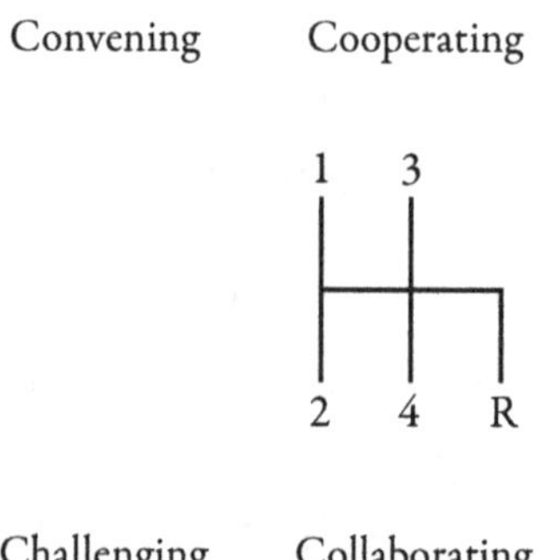


**FIGURE 14.1. THE 4-C TEAM PROCESS MODEL**

Once team process is in motion, your focus shifts to maintaining momentum toward the collaboration stage and, once there, sustaining it for as long as possible. Why this stage matters so much will become clear as we explore each of the four stages in the 4-C Model.

## A CLOSER LOOK AT THE STAGES OF THE 4-C MODEL

The first step in effectively managing team dynamics is learning to recognize the four stages of team development and identify which stage your team is currently navigating. One of the most practical and insightful ways to do this is by tuning in to the team's *central question*—the most pressing concern on their minds during each stage—and addressing it directly.

In the pages ahead, we'll explore the four stages of the 4-C Model in depth, focusing on what defines each stage, the key question that characterizes it, and how to recognize when your team is there.

### Stage 1: Convening

The convening stage of team process occurs when team members initially meet to hear about and understand their mission and goals. This stage recurs each time thereafter when the team meets to pursue them. Each of these meetings is typically marked by tentativeness and surface-level interactions during which people are trying to understand the lay of the land. They're often seeking the answers to questions, including "Who are the others here with me?" "What are we going to be trying to do?" "What's our purpose?" "When are we going to get started?"

The main question on team members' minds during the convening stage is "What are we here together to do?" Addressing this question is crucial because it helps establish psychological engagement and sets the stage for your team's active participation.

Your primary objective during the convening stage is to set direction and encourage your team's involvement. An effective technique for easing early team interactions is to use an icebreaker—a structured activity to help team members begin to get acquainted and feel comfortable (see appendix D for examples).

You'll recall that in the leadership vignette from chapter 3, Jack and his team met for the first time, received a briefing about their mission, and gathered together later in an all-night meeting to talk about what was ahead. Illustrating common convening stage behaviors, the team spent time talking about the mission they'd been assigned while simultaneously getting to know each other.

As you work with your own team, you're likely to observe similar behaviors and also many of the ones shown in table 14.1 when you're in the convening stage.

Certain specific leadership approaches and behaviors have proven to be the most and least effective in each stage of the 4-C Model. Table 14.2 outlines these for the convening stage.

## Convening Stage Pro Tips

Your team depends on you to get the ball rolling. Every time your team convenes or reconvenes, they look to you for direction. Recall from chapter 7 what Gary did at the start of class. He walked in, sat down in his chair, and set expectations, inviting students to introduce themselves in turn. By quickly making this assignment, he got his students' attention and engagement, helping them move past the "What are we doing here?" question and into action. The same goes for you every time your team convenes or reconvenes; they will look to you for direction.

### Key Takeaway

The most effective leadership action you can take in the convening stage is to get people involved quickly. You can achieve this by using

**TABLE 14.1. EXAMPLES OF TEAM MEMBER THOUGHTS, QUESTIONS, AND OBSERVABLE BEHAVIORS IN THE CONVENING STAGE**

| Team member thoughts and questions | Observable team member behaviors |
|---|---|
| What are we doing here? | Talking about surface topics, such as the weather or weekend plans |
| What's my role and others' roles? | Sharing basic personal or professional information |
| Will I be accepted? Will my ideas? | Asking about others' backgrounds |
| Who are the others on the team? | Inviting others for casual meetups |
| How much of myself will I invest? | Testing ideas to gauge reactions |
| I'm bored. | Checking out mentally |

**TABLE 14.2. EXAMPLES OF EFFECTIVE AND INEFFECTIVE LEADERSHIP BEHAVIORS IN THE CONVENING STAGE**

| Effective leadership behaviors | Ineffective leadership behaviors |
|---|---|
| Allowing people time to settle in but not too much | Pushing too fast |
| Paying attention to content and process | Being too hands-off |
| Staying alert for different versions of the "Why are we here?" question | Letting nature take its course |
| Initiating structure to get people involved and in action | Being too heavy-handed |
| Trying different approaches to get people involved and interacting while being patient | Ordering or using "Because I said so" statements |
| Preparing to shift gears into the challenging stage | Displaying anger or frustration when people aren't engaged |

an icebreaker or assigning a specific task, such as developing an agenda together. Success in the convening stage lays the foundation for productive teamwork in later stages, the next of which is the challenging stage.

## Stage 2: Challenging

The challenging stage is characterized by team members questioning roles and responsibilities, processes, and, very likely, your authority. This stage often shows up through mildly antagonistic interpersonal interactions about the best way to do certain tasks and the need to establish ground rules for behavior and set guidelines for communication.

The central two-part question people grapple with in the challenging stage is "What's my role here, and how much influence do I need to be comfortable in this team?"

Conflicts and disagreements are inevitable and may even escalate into direct confrontations involving you. We've heard some leaders say that being in the challenging stage is like trying to paddle a kayak through whitewater rapids: it can be one hell of a messy ride.

That said, remember that a bit of turbulence and conflict is a natural part of team growth, not a catastrophe. While they may be unpleasant in the moment, these difficulties serve the purpose of testing boundaries, questioning assumptions, and working out kinks in communication so the team can maintain forward motion.

Think of the energy in this stage as similar to the surge of bridled power you feel when a car shifts into second gear. Momentum is building, but it needs to be harnessed and guided.

Your role in the convening stage is to help team members find their places in the group while managing conflicts constructively. You accomplish this by staying calm, modeling active listening, and facilitating clear, nondefensive communication. Skills such as paraphrasing, redirecting interactional traffic, and teaching others how to give and receive feedback are essential. Gary demonstrated these skills during and after the altercation between Colonel House and Captain Walker, which was triggered by House's casual self-introduction. Gary remained composed, addressed the conflict directly, and later helped the entire class process the incident.

His example highlights how managing team process in the challenging stage can turn discord into dialogue—something you can become proficient at doing too. All it takes is the skilled leadership knowledge presented in this chapter and dedicated practice. See table 14.3 for examples of thoughts, questions, and behaviors and table 14.4 for specific effective and ineffective leadership behaviors during the challenging stage.

## Challenging Stage Pro Tips

This stage of team process will test your leadership mettle more than any other, but it also offers significant opportunities. Conflict, if you manage it well, can transform your team into a more cohesive and productive unit.

Your role in the challenging stage is to stay calm, listen actively, and help people communicate directly and constructively. Focus on the process, not the content of disagreements, and intervene only when you're composed and ready. Your team will notice—and appreciate—your steady leadership.

## Key Takeaway

Mastering the challenging stage requires patience, skill, and a steady focus on guiding productive interactions. Your calm presence can help ensure the kind of deeper team cohesion you'll need as you lead your team through the cooperating stage and beyond.

### TABLE 14.3. EXAMPLES OF TEAM MEMBER THOUGHTS, QUESTIONS, AND BEHAVIORS IN THE CHALLENGING STAGE

| Team member thoughts and questions | Observable team member behaviors |
|---|---|
| Who's the leader here, and why? | Challenging the leader and others |
| How influential am I? How influential could I be? | Criticizing others |
| What responsibility do I have here? | Seeking alliances with others |
| Are my needs being met? | Questioning or discussing rules or procedures |
| When are we going to stop wasting time and get to work? | Rebelling or going along |
| That person is irritating me. | Expressing displeasure |

### TABLE 14.4. EXAMPLES OF EFFECTIVE AND INEFFECTIVE LEADERSHIP BEHAVIORS IN THE CHALLENGING STAGE

| Effective leadership behaviors | Ineffective leadership behaviors |
|---|---|
| Being self-aware | Taking conflict personally |
| Observing what's happening between people | Ignoring or avoiding open conflict |
| Paying attention to content and process | Focusing only on winning arguments or being "right" |
| Staying alert for different versions of the "Why are we here?" question | Dismissing questions or shutting down differing perspectives |
| Facilitating team interactions | Allowing factions to harden or fueling "us vs. them" dynamics |
| Preparing to shift gears into the cooperating stage | Dominating the conversation or silencing certain members |

## Stage 3: Cooperating

Cooperating, as we described in chapter 2, involves people working together toward shared outcomes within their defined roles. Once your team navigates the rough spots of getting started and the natural conflicts that will always arise, and with your leadership guiding them, they'll be ready for the relative peace of the cooperating stage.

Here, team members work together more cohesively, leveraging their strengths to achieve shared goals. Cooperation is in our human DNA. As Roman emperor and Stoic philosopher Marcus Aurelius (121–180 CE) wisely noted, "We are made for cooperation, like feet, like hands, like eyelids, like the rows of the upper and lower teeth. To act against one another then is contrary to nature."[3]

In the cooperating stage, teamwork feels smoother, like the ride in your car after shifting into third gear. You experience less friction, a steady increase in momentum, and a sense of unity as the team accelerates toward its goals. The key question on people's minds in the cooperating stage is commonly "How can we support each other's strengths and move forward together?"

You witnessed an example of this kind of support in chapter 9 when Gary and Ruben met with John and Jack for a debrief of their process observation practicum. The atmosphere of safety and support in this small group led to a powerful moment of self-awareness for Jack, demonstrating the impact of a cohesive team.

Tables 14.5 and 14.6 offer a look at the cooperating stage in terms of a team's questions, thoughts, and behaviors as well as effective and ineffective leadership behaviors.

### Cooperating Stage Pro Tips

As your team begins to cooperate, your job is to keep them aligned with clear, consistent communication. Reinforce shared goals and celebrate milestones to sustain motivation. Start laying the groundwork for deeper collaboration by encouraging open dialogue and creative problem-solving. Repetition is invaluable at this stage, so keep reiterating the team's purpose and objectives.

### Key Takeaway

Cooperation sets the stage for high performance. Your role as a leader in this stage is to nurture this unity, keeping your team focused and engaged while preparing them for the more complex demands of collaboration.

**TABLE 14.5. EXAMPLES OF TEAM MEMBER THOUGHTS, QUESTIONS, AND BEHAVIORS IN THE COOPERATING STAGE**

| Team member thoughts and questions | Observable team member behaviors |
|---|---|
| I'm feeling better about this team. | Being friendly and supportive |
| I hope we don't start arguing again. | Showing increased emotional engagement |
| I like [name]. | Having friendly physical contact (fist bumps, pats on the back, and even hugs) |
| How can I contribute? | Bringing treats to share with everyone |
| Do my teammates like me? | Being open about feelings and learnings |
| I feel safe with these people. | Asking for help and having thoughtful discussions about goals |

**TABLE 14.6. EXAMPLES OF EFFECTIVE AND INEFFECTIVE LEADERSHIP BEHAVIORS IN THE COOPERATING STAGE**

| Effective leadership behaviors | Ineffective leadership behaviors |
| --- | --- |
| Reinforcing objectives and acknowledging effort and accomplishments | Pushing the team too fast |
| Celebrating progress | Being too hands-off or disengaged |
| Staying alert to process, team dynamics, and questions | Letting conflicts fester |
| Facilitating constructive interactions | Micromanaging or being overly directive |

## Stage 4: Collaborating

When your team reaches the collaborating stage, you'll observe high levels of synergy as people function together seamlessly—a phenomenon comparable to a car cruising efficiently at higher speeds in fourth gear.

Trust and mutual understanding are strong, and the team works in alignment, producing high-quality work without needing constant oversight. Openness and risk-taking abound as the question on everyone's mind becomes "What more can we do that will help us create something that we can't achieve alone?"

You saw a good example of the collaboration stage in chapter 8 when Gary and Ruben tag-teamed the explanation of the Content and Process Model. Their unrehearsed, synergistic use of short lectures and Ruben's experiential guitar demonstration created a memorable learning experience, driven by mutual trust and the freedom to improvise. See tables 14.7 and 14.8 for more examples of dialogue and behaviors during this stage.

**TABLE 14.7. EXAMPLES OF TEAM MEMBER THOUGHTS, QUESTIONS, AND BEHAVIORS IN THE COLLABORATING STAGE**

| Team member thoughts and questions | Observable team member behaviors |
|---|---|
| We're really doing something meaningful together. | Listening to each other actively |
| I don't agree with all the ideas others have, but they're all valuable. | Building on each other's ideas |
| What more can I do to help? | Giving and receiving frequent feedback |
| Let's experiment and see if this works. | Ensuring everyone is included and involved |
| I feel safe to express my opinions. | Being flexible and open to change |
| I want us all to succeed. | Celebrating successes together, large and small |

## Collaborating Stage Pro Tips

When your team is collaborating, it feels like you're a part of a well-oiled machine. People know their jobs and are doing them, trust abounds, and ideas are exchanged and acted on effortlessly.

Keep a light hand on the tiller and catch people doing the right things the right way.

## Key Takeaway

Collaboration fuels innovation and collective success. Your role in this stage is to reinforce joint effort and results with acknowledgment and praise, encourage cross-fertilization of ideas, and promote nondefensive

**TABLE 14.8. EXAMPLES OF EFFECTIVE AND INEFFECTIVE LEADERSHIP BEHAVIORS IN THE COLLABORATING STAGE**

| Effective leadership behaviors | Ineffective leadership behaviors |
|---|---|
| Encouraging participation and welcoming ideas | Pushing too fast |
| Paying attention to content and process | Being too laissez-faire |
| Asking for input, such as by asking, "What do you think? What's your opinion?" | Micromanaging |
| Modeling transparency, such as by saying, "I'm not sure, but I think it may be . . ." | Imposing decisions without input |
| Encouraging innovation, such as by saying, "Let's try this out and see what happens." | Publicly criticizing people |
| Continually talking about and encouraging collaboration | Ignoring or dismissing ideas |
| Giving and asking for feedback | Playing favorites |
| Recognizing contributions and acknowledging them publicly | Failing to address conflicts |

behaviors that facilitate the exploration of uncharted territory where breakthroughs may await.

## The Pro Tip of Leadership Pro Tips

Changes in team process can happen in the blink of an eye, and transitions between stages often happen subtly, so be observant and ready to guide your team through these shifts to keep everyone moving forward.

Here encapsulated in three short lines. is one of the simplest yet most powerful leadership frameworks you're likely to find anywhere, It provides clear guidance for effectively navigating each stage of team process, enabling you to foster alignment, manage conflict, and sustain high performance:

1. In the convening stage, initiate structure.
2. In the challenging stage, facilitate interactions.
3. In the cooperating and collaborating stages, reinforce behavior.

## A FINAL WORD ABOUT MANAGING TEAM PROCESS

Despite the many moving parts of understanding and managing team process, it's not as daunting as it may first appear. Like other parts of the Leadership Actually Model, all it takes is knowing the content of the four stages and putting in the time to practice observing, recognizing, identifying, and facilitating your team through each of them.

Can you imagine what trying to lead and manage a team would be like without some understanding of these elements and how they work together? Can you imagine a surgeon who didn't study human anatomy in medical school?

## EXTRAS: CHAPTERS 13 AND 14

### Chapters 13 and 14 Summary

- Team process is the evolving and repeating patterns of interaction—or stages of development—your team goes through as it works together over time.
- Managing team process is easily the most important piece of skilled leadership knowledge in this book.

- Although every team has and exhibits unique characteristics, all share behavioral patterns that have remained consistent across human groups throughout history.
- The skill of managing team process is often overlooked in leadership development.
- Trying to lead a team without understanding team process is like a surgeon trying to operate on people without knowledge of human anatomy.
- Extensive research supports that managing team process is fundamental to effective team leadership.[4]
- Many theories of team process (group or team development) provide only basic explanatory information with little or no practical guidance on how to manage it.
- The Leadership Actually 4-C Team Process Model is a clear explanation of what team process is, how it works, and your leadership role in managing it.
- The 4-C Team Process Model comprises four distinct stages—convening, challenging, cooperating, and collaborating—that function in ways similar to the operation of a four-speed manual transmission in a car.
- Much like learning how to drive a car with a four-speed manual transmission, the best way to learn how to manage team process is by attending experiential workshops led by experienced instructors, and then practice, practice, and practice some more.
- Neglecting team process or not knowing how to manage it is the leadership equivalent of playing Russian roulette.
- Ignoring team process can trap managers into using simplistic solutions for complex problems. As Abraham Maslow wrote, "I suppose it is tempting, if the only tool you have is a hammer, to treat everything as if it were a nail."[5]
- Managing team process is essential—and not supplementary—to your work as a leader.

- Success in managing team process hinges on your clear understanding of the Content and Process Model in chapters 7 and 8.

## How to Use the Information in Chapters 13 and 14

We have four practical suggestions for you:

- Practice. Practice. Practice.
- Print the team thoughts and behavior tables for each stage of team process, carry them with you, and use them in meetings as you observe what's happening around you.
- When you think you have a good enough grasp of the stages, use the "Effective and Ineffective Leadership Behaviors" tables for each stage and try your hand at actually managing team process with your team.
- Find and attend an experiential leadership development workshop that emphasizes managing team process.

Verse 68, *Tao Te Ching*

He who excels as a soldier is one who
Is not warlike; he who fights the best fight
Is not wrathful; he who conquers an enemy
is not quarrelsome;
he who best employs people
Is obedient himself.
This is the virtue of not-quarreling,
this is the secret of bringing out other men's ability,
this is complying with Heaven.
Since of old it is considered the greatest virtue (Te).

## Final Thoughts

We'll close this chapter as we began, by reiterating that the most important skill for you to have as a leader, and one that will more clearly distinguish you as the genuine article—is your proficiency in managing team process.

You accomplish it in two easy and ongoing steps:

1. Assess the stage of team process your team is in by using the team thoughts and behavior tables provided in this chapter.
2. Align your leadership behavior with the appropriate stage as shown in table 14.9.

**TABLE 14.9. STAGE AND EFFECTIVE BEHAVIOR ALIGNMENT**

| Stage of team process | Effective leadership behavior |
|---|---|
| Convening | Initiate structure |
| Challenging | Facilitate |
| Cooperating and collaborating | Reinforce |

It really is that easy.

# 15 "Viva la Revolución!"

> You cannot teach a man anything; you can only help him find it within himself.
>
> —Galileo Galilei

*US Army Organizational Effectiveness School. End of course.*

Graduation week finally arrived, and the sixteen-week OE course was nearing its end. Most of Gary's students had expected this would be a time of celebration and new beginnings. Instead, they found themselves in a reflective and conflicted mood.

On one hand, they were excited to move forward with their lives. On the other, they were anxious about whether they were truly ready to apply what they'd learned. Did they know enough? Would they be able to perform? Would the larger army recognize and utilize their new OE skills, or would they just be seen as curiosities—living symbols of another out-of-step program of the month?

In this reflective state, they began to take stock. They had no doubt gained knowledge, understanding, and skills. Some had even developed a new philosophical outlook—one that recognized soldiers not just as soldiers but as human beings, who were capable of almost infinite good when their leaders provided them with authentic, effective, and purpose-driven leadership.

Alongside these gains, they had experienced painful losses. Marriages dissolved under the weight of personal change. Friendships grew distant, and in many cases, the comforting simplicity of their previous worldviews had been replaced by an awareness that was at once enlightening and burdensome.

Their insights into human interaction made returning to the familiar routines of the past fundamentally incompatible. Their new awareness of themselves and others, as well as the ever-present dynamics of leading, all contributed to a sense of dissonance and unease in the group.

As they grappled with these feelings and their imminent return to the regular army, questions from the first morning resurfaced: "What am I doing here? What have I gotten myself into?" They were back in the convening stage.

But just as he did on the first morning of the course, Gary had kept a watchful eye. He heard whispers of his students' unease. Sensing that they were at a pivotal moment, he sprang into action, arranging a hasty meeting.

As the students filed into Gary's classroom, they stopped short, their eyes drawn to a banner that stretched across the front wall, its bold lettering demanding their attention: "Non puoi insegnare niente a un uomo. Puoi solo aiutarlo a scoprire ciò che ha dentro di sé."

Some exchanged puzzled glances. A few tried to guess its meaning. Gary entered, his eyes twinkling at their confusion. "I see you've noticed my banner," he said, grinning. "It's Italian, attributed to Galileo during the Renaissance. It means 'You cannot teach a man anything. You can only help him find it within himself.'"

He paused, letting the students consider its meaning. "I read it recently, and it got me thinking. That's why I wanted us to get together today."

Taking a breath, he said, "I'd like to hear what you consider the most important thing you've discovered within yourselves over these past few months. What stands out?" With that, class was back in session. Gary gave them one of his signature two-part assignments:

"Part one: Take fifteen minutes to think quietly. Identify the three most important things you've learned about yourself during this course.

"Then, part two: Pair up and discuss your thoughts for thirty minutes. Afterward, take a short break, and we'll get back together for a discussion."

The discussions that ensued after the break were lively and spirited. Laughter punctuated the hour, and time flew by. When he sensed the discussion was over, Gary began. "So tell me. What have you discovered within yourselves? What have been your biggest learnings? Bob and Norm, it seems appropriate that you should lead us off. After all, it was you two who got the ball rolling on our first morning together."

The room burst into laughter. Without hesitation, Bob—Captain Walker—smirked as he pointed at Colonel House and said wryly, "I discovered it was okay to call my good friend Colonel House—yes, you, sir—Norm."

The group laughed again.

"Seriously, though," Walker continued, his tone softening, "I've learned how to relate to people, not just to their ranks and titles. I understand the power of content and process. And, probably most of all, I really get how vital interdependence is in teams. The experience of these last few months has changed me immeasurably. Thank you, everyone." Visibly moved, he glanced around the group, his eyes lingering on Gary.

Eyes glistening, Gary nodded. "Thanks, Bob. You've grown in ways we all can see." He let the sentiment linger before turning to Norm, who, straightening in his chair, began thoughtfully. "I've worn this uniform a lot of years. If only this course had existed when I was a junior officer . . . what a difference it would've made. Looking at all of you who I've gotten to know so well, I can't help thinking about the impact you're going to make.

"As for me, my wife says I'm a better listener now." Laughter pealed through the room. "I've also learned how to give and receive feedback—skills I never thought I'd master. The OE course has been one of the most amazing experiences of my life. Thank you all."

The next student in the queue, soft-spoken John Capriccio, Jack's process observation practicum partner from chapter 9, talked about learning the four-step OE process: assessment, planning, implementation, and evaluation or follow-up. "I can use it everywhere in my life, not just at work," he said, enthusiasm evident in his voice.

He went on to mention the value of learning how to design experiential workshops before pausing, gathering his courage. "But the most important thing I've learned is how to ask for and accept help. I used to be a lone wolf, but with your help, I now understand what a team is for." He stood and walked the circle, shaking hands with each of his classmates and Gary and Ruben, a ritual of gratitude that left no one unmoved.

One by one, the students shared, until only Jack remained. Shifting in his seat, he began, uncharacteristically vulnerable. "I realized . . . I'm more than the tough, no-nonsense officer I've pretended to be since coming back from Vietnam. I can be real now, especially with my family." He swallowed hard. "And the power of how . . . is something I'll never forget."

He hesitated and added haltingly, "The way I feel right now must be how wounded wild animals feel after they've been rescued, treated, healed, and are about to be released back into the wild. I'm terrified." His voice cracked with a raw honesty that resonated with everyone in the room. Gary nodded, his gaze steady, offering quiet solidarity.

"Thanks, everyone," Gary said, preparing to move on. But before he could say another word, he was interrupted by a chorus of voices.

"Whoa, wait a minute, *Doctor* Drexler. Not so fast! What about you and Ruben? We want to know what you two discovered too!"

Gary laughed, shaking his head. "I should've known we can't get away with anything in this group anymore." He composed himself, looked at Ruben, and said, "I'll go first. What I've learned—actually relearned working with all of you—is something I first learned from Carl Rogers when I worked for him at the Center for Studies of the Person in La Jolla. It's a lesson about learning through experience, not books or lectures."

He let his words land, then continued. "This type of learning is called experiential or empirical learning, which is how adults learn best—by learning through doing. We've practiced experiential learning from day one of the course, and you're going to use it to help reshape and reinvigorate learning in the army.

"Experiential learning is the future, and you're about to launch it into low earth orbit. You're leaving here to become teachers, do applied research in the field, and, above all, continue to learn. How far-out is that?"

He grinned. "But you know what? That's not what excites me the most. The best thing of all is that you're all about to become guerrilla revolutionaries—institutional guerrillas who'll spark positive change in the army from the inside out.

"You'll be in the field practicing OE, doing applied research, and learning. It's my hope, and the school's, that you'll feed your lessons learned back to us here so we can incorporate them into the curriculum for the classes that follow you. Together, we'll be paying it forward and shaping generations of army leaders far into the future.

"You're all about to make a monumental contribution to help revolutionize learning and growth in one of the largest and most calcified organizations in the world. I can't think of anything more important!"

His voice rising, he raised his fist and shouted, "Congratulations! You're prepared! You're ready! Viva la revolución!"

The classroom erupted in cheers.

# 16 Teaching and Learning Together

> Were all instructors to realize that the quality of mental process, not the production of correct answers, is the measure of educative growth something hardly less than a revolution in teaching would be worked.
>
> —John Dewey

Like the medieval cartographer who marked the uncharted territories on his globes with the foreboding phrase *Hic sunt dracones* ("Here be dragons"), John Dewey embraced the timeless human desire to explore the unknown, setting out to redefine education and transform how people learn.

Humanity's enthusiasm for discovery continues today, spanning work from the examination of our human past through archaeology and our present in neuroscience and consciousness studies to our future in the ongoing exploration of space. This unquenchable thirst for discovery is probably best encapsulated in the fictional universe of *Star Trek*, where Starfleet's mission is to "boldly go where no one has gone before."

Educators like Dewey were masters of this spirit, paving the way for a new era of teaching and learning. As you've seen, Gary Drexler was a visionary educator in his own right. He foresaw the need for a transformation in how military leaders were taught and became one of his field's most passionate practitioners.

Whether in the military or on the frontlines of your workplace, venturing into the unknown and trying out new ways of operating always requires courage, curiosity, and a commitment to continuous learning.

To support these requirements, this chapter continues to explore the transformation in teaching and learning that Gary embodied and helped to pioneer at the army's OE school. We'll trace where these passions have been, where they are now, and where they're headed next and then discuss how you can carry them forward in your work today.

## WHERE EDUCATION HAS BEEN

In his seminal work *The Modern Practice of Adult Education,* pioneering American educator Dr. Malcolm Knowles described the origins of pedagogy (the art and science of teaching) in sixth-century Europe.[1] Monks created this approach to teach youngsters enrolled in monastic schools how to read and write.

This highly effective model endured for centuries, embedding itself in both church-sponsored and nonreligious schools, eventually reshaping universities and other institutions of higher learning worldwide.

Until the mid-1700s, education functioned primarily as a vehicle for training the workforce, equipping children and young adults with the necessary skills and indoctrinating them so as to fit seamlessly into society's labor demands. Teaching and learning evolved into largely transactional processes, prioritizing memorization and the rote regurgitation of facts over genuine understanding. The overarching goal was to ensure cultural continuity—embedding ideologies, customs, and values to uphold the status quo.

The Industrial Revolution of the eighteenth and nineteenth centuries ushered in an era of complex machinery, mass production, and economic transformation, dramatically altering the educational landscape. Schooling could no longer simply transmit traditional ways of working; it needed to adapt and evolve. It had to supply a steady stream of workers who could read, write, and perform basic arithmetic—skills critical to the new industrial economy. It fulfilled these needs admirably, laying the foundations of our modern world.

As the twentieth century began, visionary educators Dewey and Knowles recognized the limitations of the Industrial Age educational model. Its rigid, formulaic processes stifled independent thought and hindered people's ability to function effectively in modern life's increasing complexities.

Dewey believed that education is a social process that should prepare students for active citizenship by developing social skills such as collaboration, communication, and a sense of community. Knowles further emphasized that "adults are most interested in learning subjects that have immediate relevance to their job or personal life."[2]

Among influential educators, Knowles had perhaps the most influence in workplace education, introducing the concept and practice of andragogy—"the art and science of teaching adults."[3] His ideas helped revolutionize education at a time when, after the two world wars and decades of hierarchical control, people were eager for change.

Predictably, one of the first places these changes began was in the classroom, as educators started to revolutionize educational methodologies across every age group. As you saw in chapter 15, Gary Drexler was at the forefront of putting these ideas into practice in, of all places, the US Army.

## WHERE EDUCATION IS TODAY

Today, the revolution in education Gary described to his OE students is picking up steam. We are shifting away from outdated, factory-style teaching methods.

The sun is setting on the era of rigid, inflexible, classroom-based learning that focused on the transmission of information and cultural conformity. In its place, more dynamic, pragmatic, and flexible models are emerging. Lessons that once revolved around policies and rules now emphasize engagement, exploration, and hands-on experience. Traditional teaching and learning methods centered on acquiring knowledge and skills through instruction and individual study have evolved into more holistic and team-based processes.

These and other innovative approaches emphasize reflection, absorption, integration, and practical application to foster deep and lasting understanding.

Another telling marker of the revolution is that in many places, the classroom is no longer confined to a physical space. The classroom is more of a mindset—a way of thinking—that feels equally at home in a factory breakroom, in a huddle gathered around a piece of machinery, or during a hands-on demo of the latest large language model release as it does in a state-of-the-art classroom.

For example, GE CEO Larry Culp's gemba walks from chapter 12 embody the idea of a free-range learner mindset. By directly observing and engaging with employees on the factory floor, GE leaders break down traditional barriers to connection and learning.

At an even deeper level, these walks reflect our often-overlooked human preference for physical proximity to our leaders, a key element in building trust and promoting collaboration.

The central reason for the successes of the revolution in education is that the new approaches to it recognize and are based on the realities of human nature. While we're generally open to experimentation, most of us ultimately choose what we know works over what may not.

What works in teaching and learning is the communication and transfer of skilled knowledge that's relevant to and designed around the tasks we're accountable to do by virtue of the roles we occupy.

Equally effective is guiding, mentoring, and nurturing people's overall growth and development. We humans have an abiding and deep-seated yearning to fulfill our individual potentials and contribute them in some way to the good of the whole.

It's not an accident if teaching and learning together sounds similar to leadership. Teaching, learning, and leading all stem from the same innate human drive to create, connect, and grow. Conversely, clinging to outdated methods—embodied in the oft-heard phrase "But we've always done it this way"—undermines progress and innovation.

Today, both exemplary teaching and genuine leadership prioritize assessment, collaboration, pilot-testing, and facilitation in the advancement of education. Additionally, they encourage leaders, teachers, and learners to co-create dynamic environments driven by necessity and invention.

We'd like to highlight two crucial pieces of background involving necessity and invention. First, your role as a leader places you at the heart of the ongoing revolution in teaching and learning—the very one Gary passionately shared with his students. Second, contributing to this revolution requires unprecedented levels of openness, creativity, and inventiveness in how you lead and teach.

## THE REVOLUTION IS HERE

The revolution in education isn't coming. It's already knocking at your door. New opportunities are emerging for you as a leader as the traditional classroom-based learning model continues to evolve and grow.

Around the globe, the demand for adult learning far outpaces the availability of teachers and classrooms. On the surface, this might seem like a simple numbers game: too many learners, not enough teachers. But the real issue goes deeper.

It's not just about how many teachers we have or even how skilled they are. The real challenge lies in how education is delivered. Far too often, traditional systems fail to equip people with the tools they need to thrive in the real world, leaving them disconnected from both their potential and their purpose.

As William Deresiewicz, a former professor at Yale and Columbia, starkly observed, even graduates from elite universities often leave feeling unprepared for life beyond the classroom—disillusioned by an education that prioritized theory over practical value.[4]

This same frustration echoes in the workplace. According to Gallup's *State of the Global Workplace Report 2023,* 67 percent of workers feel disengaged.[5] Both groups—underprepared graduates and disengaged employees—have something in common: a profound sense of disconnection and a longing for positive change.

## WHAT DO THEY REALLY WANT?

As a leader, teacher, and changemaker, you may feel tempted to ask, "What is this positive change that will bridge the disconnection, and how do I deliver it?" Many people will tell you, "I just want to be empowered."

But here's where the situation gets tricky. This seemingly simple answer often leads down a rabbit hole, not unlike Alice's tumble into Wonderland—confusing, disorienting, and full of contradictions.

The real problem lies in how empowerment is understood and pursued. To address the two-pronged issue of disconnectedness and the longing for positive change, you'll need to grapple with both challenges at the same time—much like you might've done in math class, but this time solving a pair of metaphorical versus algebraic simultaneous equations.

First, the word *empowerment* has become a cliché. Overused and stripped of clarity, it's like a dull knife that can no longer cut through the complexities of what people truly seek. In its vagueness, it has come to mean everything and nothing at the same time.

Second, far too many people believe empowerment is something that must be granted by someone else. They see it as something—authority, permission, or validation—that's to be delivered to them by someone or some entity outside of themselves. This mindset leaves them stuck, wasting valuable time waiting for someone to hand them what they could and should be cultivating or already have within themselves. Think of the characters Dorothy, the Scarecrow, the Tin-Man, and the Cowardly Lion from *The Wizard of Oz*.

These intertwined issues create a paradox for you in your role as a leader to sort out: (a) a word that has lost its meaning still wields immense power over people's sense of fulfillment and (b) the fact that you need to teach them about the glorious gift they already possess but don't know how to unwrap—their own self-efficacy.

## EMPOWERMENT: A NEW PERSPECTIVE

What's the answer to this paradox? How do you break the cycle and help others stop chasing their tails? Here are a few steps you can take.

The first step is to retire the term *empowerment* and recast it as *personal agency*, which is the self-directed capacity to make decisions, act, and take responsibility for the outcomes. Agency isn't something you give others but rather something you teach them about, facilitate, and foster.

The second step is to encourage agency in your team. You do that by creating the conditions where agency can flourish. This starts with building trust and safety and allowing people to take risks and explore their potential without fear of failure. It's like teaching someone to swim: what they need most in the beginning is to muster the courage to let go of the side of the pool so they'll eventually be able to venture into deeper water.

Agency thrives in an environment where people feel encouraged to experiment, fail, and grow. When you focus on fostering agency, you empower people in the truest sense—not by granting permission but by equipping them with the mindset and tools to succeed on their own terms. This is the revolution you're being called to lead. Will you answer the knock at the door?

## THE ROAD TO AGENCY

Like any meaningful journey, the path to agency rarely follows a straight line. It winds through engagement—the level of involvement and enthusiasm people feel about their work[6]—and finds its footing in shared purpose, respect, and collaboration.

Few approaches are as effective at fostering engagement and agency in teaching and learning together. This strategy opens a world of possibilities for team development and organizational growth as you inspire creativity and innovation within your team, turning challenges into transformative learning experiences.

In the spirit of starting small, here are three easy and reliable ways to promote engagement and agency in the context of teaching and learning together:

- Conduct interviews with participants before training sessions or other events.
- Involve people in the design of training or events.
- Leverage the protégé effect by encouraging team members to teach one another.

Let's explore each of these in more detail, before diving into a real-world example of these ideas in action.

### Conduct Interviews before Training or Other Events

Engagement begins with listening. One-to-one interviews with participants before a training session or event are an excellent way to set the tone. These conversations allow you to learn about their expectations, background, learning preferences, and goals.

The benefits are twofold. First, the insights you gain help you tailor the content, pacing, and delivery of your training to better suit your audience. Second, these interviews create positive anticipation, generate buzz, and signal to people that their input is valued. People naturally feel more invested when they are asked for their opinions, making this a simple yet powerful tool for engagement.

## Involve Participants in Training or Event Design

For some, the idea of involving participants in training or event design can feel risky. It might seem like relinquishing control, but this is far from the case. Inviting input doesn't mean ceding decision-making power. It means modeling collaboration.

By involving your team, you build trust, confidence, and goodwill while fostering a sense of shared ownership. This process creates a developmental opportunity for everyone involved, showing that their voices matter and that leadership is at least as much about listening as it is about directing.

## Use the Protégé Effect—Encourage People to Teach

The Roman philosopher Seneca said, "While we teach, we learn." He was right. The phenomenon known as the protégé effect occurs when people teach others and they find that doing so also deepens their own understanding. When people are tasked with explaining a concept to colleagues, they tend to think more critically, identify more gaps in their knowledge, and engage more deeply with the material.

Encouraging employees to teach one another not only reinforces learning but also fosters a culture of mutual respect and collaboration. Using the protégé effect can help you transform the way your team grows and learns together.

While proactive approaches like these can be helpful, you know from experience that unexpected challenges have a nasty habit of coming your way when you least expect them. When they do, we like to remember a quote from best-selling author Rick Warren: "Life is a series of problem-solving opportunities. The problems you face will either defeat you or develop you depending on how you respond to them."[7]

## BUILDING AN AGENCY-BASED CULTURE: A CASE STUDY

Below is a particularly striking example of Warren's quote in action. It comes from our project at a wholesale distribution center (DC) in Northern California when what began as a minor issue escalated into a crisis that threatened operations, employee morale, and the DC's relationships with its customers. We offer the story to you as an example of how to build a personal agency–based culture.

### Background and Setting

Our client was the general manager of a medium-sized DC whose mission was to store and move products between the parent company's suppliers and retail customers.

Like most distribution centers, our client's facility was arranged physically into zoned areas, including receiving (loading docks), storage (aisles of floor-to-ceiling racks that were further subdivided into rows and bins), picking and packing (stations for selecting and packaging items for shipment), and shipping (where outbound packages are consolidated and loaded onto transport vehicles).

The facility employed approximately 250 people working as inventory specialists, forklift operators, order pickers, quality inspectors, and shipping coordinators in a three-shift operation.

The overarching goals of this compact workforce were minimizing handling time and storage costs while maximizing throughput and ensuring the right products reached the right customers in good condition.

## The Incident

The trouble began when one of the DC's day shift supervisors publicly berated several pickers for errors in order accuracy. He accused them of being lazy and indifferent to their work. Unsurprisingly, tensions flared, and trust within the team eroded. Within days, the conflict spilled over and out of the facility proper, drawing the attention of a local union, which issued a formal letter of intent to organize.

For a company that prided itself on being an employer of choice, the situation was dire. Faced with a rapidly worsening crisis, the general manager took decisive action, engaging us to help him figure out how to deal with the immediate threat of unionization, then work with him to devise a positive, longer-term strategy.

## The Resolution

Resolving the immediate conflict required swift and decisive measures. The supervisor was reprimanded, and employee concerns were quickly addressed through an extensive, round-the-clock pro-employee communications campaign.

As a result of his wide-ranging meetings with employees, the general manager was able to see beyond the immediate crisis and envision a workplace culture built on agency, collaboration, and mutual growth. His bold idea was to align profitability with employee development, creating an environment where people thrived alongside the organization.

Working together with our team and the DC's employees, the general manager launched the Facility Development Program (FDP), built on a simple yet powerful principle: education as a catalyst for engagement and agency.

## The Aftermath

The DC manager's commitment to fostering a workplace grounded in learning and growth turned out to be a transformative decision. Employees were invited to participate in leadership training, co-design short training courses, and engage in hands-on professional development.

The FDP's first initiative, Business Awareness Training (BAT), taught employees how to read and interpret the DC's monthly profit and loss statement, which helped them connect their daily work to the company's overall profitability.

But what made BAT really unique was its collaborative design. For example, the facility's accounting manager worked with employees to create a curriculum that emphasized the financial and customer service impact of their roles.

Additionally, rather than relying on lectures or reading, BAT encouraged active learning. Employees engaged directly in discussions and exercises, making the connection between their work and the organization's broader goals.

BAT's capstone was the creation of small BAT Teams, a name employees embraced with enthusiasm, often drawing playful comparisons to the iconic superhero. These teams visited customers, gathered feedback, and presented actionable insights to improve operations. By linking their daily efforts to customer satisfaction and company success, employees experienced a tangible sense of purpose and accountability.

## The Outcomes

The results of the FDP were extraordinary. Employee engagement in the DC soared, operational errors dropped by 35 percent, and the facility achieved over $500,000 in cost savings within just six months.

As a gesture of commitment to the course of action the DC had collaboratively charted, the DC general manager publicly presented the company CEO a check for half a million dollars, representing the savings generated by the program to date.

The FDP quickly captured the attention of the company's leadership, up to and including the board of directors, who, inspired by the FDP's results in a single facility, became sponsors of its expansion across all sixty-plus of the company's DCs.

The Northern California facility became a model for how education and agency can drive both personal and organizational growth, with many of its employees acting as coaches for their counterparts in sister DCs throughout the United States.

### Lessons Learned

This case study demonstrates how an internally driven people-centered approach to workplace challenges can transform teams, facilities, and even entire companies. By reframing problems as opportunities and focusing on personal agency, collaboration, and shared learning, virtually anyone can unlock untapped potential and achieve remarkable results.

## SHARE YOUR STORY

We'd love to hear your stories of innovation and growth. How are you and your team using teaching and learning to build agency and engagement? Whether through hands-on training or other creative approaches, we invite you to share your experiences with us at www.ccla-co.com. Let's work together to redefine what's possible when leaders and teams collaborate to reach their full potential.

## EXTRAS: CHAPTERS 15 AND 16

### Chapters 15 and 16 Summary

- An ongoing revolution in teaching and learning encourages a learning leadership approach that embraces uncertainty and ambiguity.
- This revolution employs strategies and methods that are very different from the formal educational methods of teaching children that began in the monastic schools of sixth-century Europe.
- The organized teaching of children is called pedagogy. The approach, when it began, was so successful it was adopted widely across educational institutions at every level.
- Up through the Industrial Age, education was primarily about preparing children for work and transferring cultural norms through memorization and rigid curricula.
- The focus began to shift to andragogy, experientially based and job-related adult education, in the early twentieth century.
- Educators and psychologists joined together to emphasize the importance of the learner's experience and the practical application of knowledge.[8]
- In many places today, rigid, formal classroom-based teaching and learning has given way to flexible, pragmatic approaches, such as breakroom workshops, hands-on demos, and gemba walks.
- In such places, teaching and learning is increasingly rooted in involvement, reflection, and practical application in environments that prioritize assessment, design, testing, and facilitation.
- Even with supplemental help from online learning, microlearning, mobile learning, and other approaches, the current educational system cannot meet the vast demands for practical teaching and learning in the workplace.
- As a leader, you have a huge opportunity to step in and fill this gap by doing the following:

    - Finding ways to blur the line between working and learning
    - Integrating teaching into how you work with your team
    - Promoting engagement and personal agency through your instruction
- Three proven strategies can help you put a new teaching and learning leadership approach into practice:
    - Involve participants ahead of time by using interviews before the meeting or event begins.
    - Invite participants to collaborate with you in designing and developing training or other events.
    - Use the protégé effect and provide opportunities for participants to teach.

## How to Use the Information in Chapters 15 and 16

The next time you're planning to do a training, an important meeting, or an event, consider doing one-to-one interviews with participants. You'll find a list of generic sample questions in appendix E.

Verse 27, *Tao Te Ching*

Good walkers leave no tracks,
good speakers make no errors,
good counters need no abacus,
good wardens have no need for
bolts and locks for no one can
get by them. Good binders can
dispense with rope and cord, yet
none can unloose their hold.
Therefore the wise man trusting in
goodness always saves men,

for there is no outcast to him.
Trusting in goodness he saves all things
for there is nothing valueless to him.
This is recognizing concealed values.
Therefore the good man is the instructor
of the evil man, and the evil man is the
good man's wealth.
He who does not esteem his instructors
or value his wealth, though he be otherwise
intelligent, becomes confused.
Herein lies the significance of spirituality.

## Final Thoughts

***US Army Organizational Effectiveness School. Last day of class.***

By the end of the OE course, the students realized that their mission was to help the army train for and fight wars more effectively.

This stark truth troubled some of them, Jack included. He wrestled with his growing conviction that war was senseless—particularly now that he believed he'd glimpsed one way to help prevent it: through teaching people how to work together more effectively.

Jack wasn't naive; he understood the need for armies, the principles they embodied, and the deterrent power they represented. Still, he questioned whether he wanted—or ought—to be a part of it.

Perhaps as a gesture of gratitude or as a reflection of his emerging ideals, Jack crafted a small, colorful stained-glass suncatcher in the shape of a peace symbol. He made it one evening in a class on Monterey's Fisherman's Wharf he and his wife enrolled in as a way to spend time together and give them both a rare escape from the intensity of the OE course.

Gary's OE students gathered for one last celebration following their graduation ceremony. Glasses of wine in hand, they exchanged farewells filled with laughter, hugs, claps on the back, and tears.

The atmosphere brimmed with camaraderie and mutual respect among classmates including George Taylor, Russ Smith, Bob Walker, Norm House, John Capriccio, Wally Claussen, and others. Members of the school's faculty and staff were also present: Gary, Ruben, and others. A shared sense of purpose and accomplishment bound them all together.

Amid the goodbyes, Jack approached Gary—the man he considered his first mentor—and quietly handed him a small, gift-wrapped package. Inside was the fragile piece of gleaming glass shaped into the peace symbol—the universal emblem of the ideals Jack was beginning to hold dear. This gift was his way of expressing both his gratitude to Gary and the contradictions he was still grappling with.

Decades later, this tiny gift would resurface as a poignant reminder of the most formative period in Jack's life and the leader and teacher who had helped shape it. The peace symbol, fragile yet enduring, carried the weight of Jack's journey and the lessons of a mentor who'd helped him see the world differently.

In the final chapter pair, we'll explore the fourth stage of the 4-C Team Process Model: collaboration. Within this stage lies the true pinnacle of teamwork—co-creation—where individuals work together to achieve outcomes far greater than what any could accomplish alone. Stay with us as we delve into how you can foster this extraordinary level of collaboration and take your leadership to new heights.

# 17 It's Not Rocket Science

However much you know giraffes, to see one in the wild for the first time feels prehistoric.

—Jane Goodall

*Fort Lewis, Washington. 1976, a few weeks later.*

At this point in his life, Jack didn't know anything about giraffes or have a clue about who Jane Goodall was. Her groundbreaking work with chimpanzees at Gombe Stream National Park in Tanzania probably escaped his notice too. But Jack would have related wholeheartedly to her sentiment about encountering a giraffe in the wild because he had a "giraffe" in his life too—his very first OE client. Here's the story.

As the OE course drew to a close, an administrative glitch in the army's assignments machinery left Jack facing a thirty-day gap between graduation and his report date at his new duty station in Germany. He was given two options: take thirty days of leave or stay on at the OE school as a gofer, running errands for the faculty. Neither suited him, so true to form, he started looking for other out-of-the-box alternatives. As he did, his thoughts kept returning to a telephone conversation he'd had recently with his good friend and brother-in-arms, Captain Egan Samad.

Samad and Jack had first met as lieutenants, their easy camaraderie forged in the long hours of shared duty. Now, years later, Samad's voice carried a mix of pride and unease over the phone. He'd just been promoted to operations officer—S3 in army speak—of his artillery battalion at Fort Lewis. "It's a big step up," Samad admitted. Although he welcomed more responsibility, the timing couldn't have been worse, and a knot of anxiety tightened in his chest every time he thought about all that lay ahead.

What gave Samad the most concern was the battalion's upcoming annual Army Training and Evaluation Program—ARTEP. In just two months, they would face one of the army's most rigorous proficiency tests, and as operations officer, it would fall on Samad's shoulders to ensure a passing grade. Failure was not an option. The battalion had already failed twice in as many years, and both prior operations officers—seasoned majors—had been relieved of duty. Samad refused to be the third.

"There's no way I'm going to complete a hat trick of failures," Samad said with a dry laugh.

Jack smiled through the phone at his friend's defiance. This was the Samad he knew and admired: a leader who thrived under pressure and refused to back down from a challenge.

This wasn't the first time Samad had faced adversity. As a cadet at West Point, he captained the academy's wrestling squad to victory, earning a well-deserved reputation as a fierce competitor and inspirational leader. He lived by the words inscribed over the entrance to the campus gymnasium, a quote from General of the Army Douglas MacArthur: "On the fields of friendly strife are sown the seeds that upon other fields on other days will bear the fruits of victory."[1] That grit and determination carried Samad through tough times before. He just had to summon it again.

When their call ended, no solutions had been reached, but both men felt better. Samad had lightened his burden by sharing it with someone he trusted, and Jack had reminded his friend of the strength within him. For now, that was enough.

With Samad left thinking about the ARTEP, Jack still had some ruminating of his own to do. How was he going to solve his predicament of the aggravating break between assignments? As he turned it over in his mind, his thoughts kept coming back to Samad's ARTEP challenge. The more he pondered it, the more he felt a familiar pull—not just the lure of helping solve a difficult problem but also the sense that he might be on the threshold of something bigger, something momentous.

One evening over burgers and beers with his wife, Ellen, an idea took shape. He asked her, "What do you think of me offering to help Egan prepare for his upcoming ARTEP? Could I use the skills I've learned at the OE school to help make a difference in such a short time? If Egan agrees, I'd be able to do something meaningful before we head to Germany. I could help him and test whether OE works in a real unit."

Ever the grounded one, Ellen said, "Why not, Jack? It sounds positive all the way around. I have confidence in you and in Egan and think this idea will work." By the time they left the restaurant, his mind was made up. The next morning, he called Samad.

"Egan, hear me out. What if I came back up to Fort Lewis before I head overseas and helped you prep for the ARTEP? We'd put some of this OE mumbo jumbo I've been learning to the test, see if it actually works in the real world—or if it's just academic fluff. Worst case, it bombs, and we go back to prepping the good old army way. But if it works, we nail this thing. What do you say?"

Samad didn't hesitate. "Jack, are you serious? You'd do that for me?"

"Of course I'm serious. What do you think?"

"Hell yes!" Samad said, his voice charged with a mix of gratitude and determination. "Let's make it happen!"

Jack hung up and smiled. He didn't know exactly how things would play out, but one thing was certain: the next thirty days wouldn't be dull. The ARTEP challenge was about to begin.

## THE ARTEP CHALLENGE

To understand the ARTEP, think of it like the rigorous certification processes in industries like healthcare or nuclear energy. Just as the staffs of hospitals or nuclear plants must prove they know what they're doing to remain operational, many army units also face uncompromising tests to prove their readiness for combat.

For the artillery in Jack's day, the ARTEP was a muscled-up, multi-day field training exercise designed to test the combined mettle of men, methods, and machines under the stress of simulated but realistic round-the-clock combat operations. The ultimate measure of success would be delivering timely and accurate fire—"steel on target"—downrange.

Doing so required the seamless coordination of brains and brawn. The brawn was supplied by soldiers who manned, loaded, and fired an artillery unit's weapons, typically called *howitzers*. The brains belonged to a small team of highly numerate soldiers in the fire direction center (FDC), whose job it was to solve what's called the *gunnery problem*—an intricate set of calculations that factored in distance, altitude, weather, and more. The result ensured that the artillery shells, once fired, hit their targets with deadly precision.

Despite the introduction of digital computers into FDCs in the early 1970s, many FDC teams clung to manual methods they trusted more. After all, they'd trained for years with slide rules, protractors, and charts. Old habits die hard.

But technology versus tradition wasn't the only hurdle. The real challenge of the ARTEP was performing under the worst possible conditions—on the move, in the dead of night under blackout conditions, through freezing rain or scorching heat, with hungry and sleep-deprived soldiers stretched to their limits. Precision was expected no matter what the odds.

For Samad's battalion, those odds felt even steeper. With two consecutive failures hanging over them, success this time wasn't just about passing the test; it was about restoring pride and confidence. And with Jack's arrival and an unconventional plan taking shape, the stakes were about to get even higher.

## A PLAN TAKES SHAPE

When Jack arrived at Fort Lewis, he went straight to Samad's office. Within minutes, they were strategizing. Jack, fresh from his OE training, introduced two OE principles he believed might revolutionize ARTEP preparation:

- People support what they help create.
- The classroom isn't a place; it's a mindset.

Samad, as scary smart as ever, quickly grasped their significance. "So instead of boring my team to death with classroom lectures, you're saying that we get them involved—turn preparation into something they help design?"

"Exactly!" Jack exclaimed.

Samad slapped his leg. "Hot damn, Jack! It's not rocket science, is it? Let's do it!"

## NAIL THE ARTEP

They shook hands and energized, headed to lunch where they sketched a high-level three-step outline of a plan on the back of a napkin, shown in figure 17.1. They called the plan "Nail the ARTEP." Jack, a black-belt pack rat, swears he still has that napkin somewhere in his files.

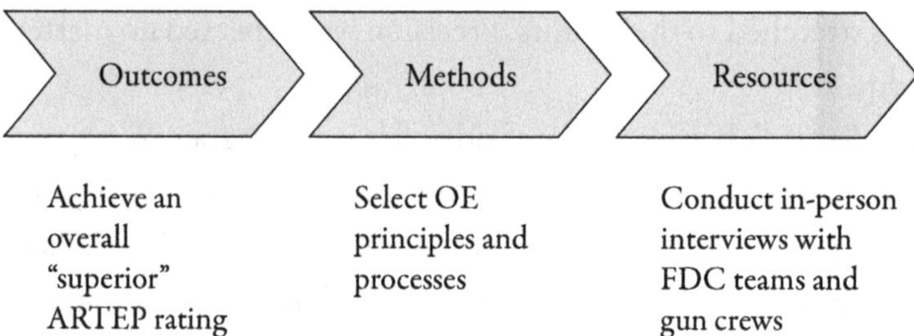


**FIGURE 17.1. NAIL THE ARTEP**

When the friends returned to Samad's office, buoyed by their earlier discussions, they immediately began fleshing out a more detailed seven-step process, illustrated in figure 17.2.

At first glance, the process plan may look like a simple flowchart, but digging a little deeper, you can see it was a carefully considered approach rooted in OE principles.

As Samad and Jack moved from ideas to implementation, they focused on creating a process that not only addressed the immediate challenge of the ARTEP but also fostered a sense of ownership and buy-in among the soldiers. Here's a brief recap of each step of the process plan that they put together.

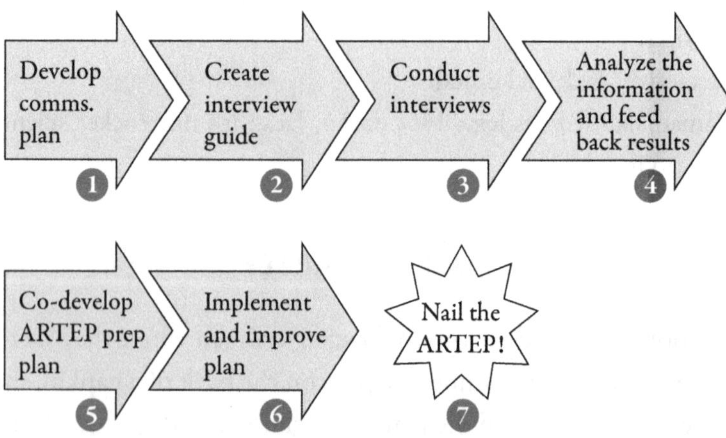


**FIGURE 17.2. NAIL THE ARTEP PREP PROCESS PLAN**

## 1. Develop a Communications Plan

The first step in the plan was to develop a communications plan—not to issue orders but to ensure awareness and understanding across the entire team and begin to create a shared vision that everyone could rally around.

## 2. Create an Interview Guide

Next, they crafted an interview guide designed to systematically gather input from team members. This step was crucial for maintaining consistency and ensuring that the feedback they received was both relevant and actionable.

The goal was to tap into the collective insights of the soldiers, setting the stage for informed decision-making. To make the guide even more effective, they sent it to the soldiers they'd be interviewing ahead of time.

## 3. Conduct Interviews

The interview guide in hand, Samad and Jack conducted one-to-one interviews, creating an environment where soldiers could speak openly without fear of reprisal. This step was about more than just collecting data. It built trust and showed people that everyone's opinion mattered.

Samad and Jack both sat in on and observed a few of one another's interviews and then met afterward to share feedback: what went well and what needed to be tweaked. They wanted to make sure the interviews accomplished what they needed them to do.

Observing Samad talk with his soldiers, Jack was struck by how effortless the conversations seemed—brimming with mutual respect, trust, and comradeship. The mood in the interview room was simultaneously personal and professional. "How does Egan do that? What's his magic?" Jack wondered. He made a mental note to think more about it.

He didn't realize it in that moment, but a year later in a meeting with his new CO in Germany, he'd get an insight into Samad's magic in the most extraordinary way.

### 4. Analyze the Information and Feed Back the Results

Once the interviews were completed, responses were aggregated and analyzed, resulting in a list of findings that were shared with the team. This step was the critical juncture where information is turned into communication and action. By feeding back the results, Samad and Jack encouraged open discussion, ensuring next steps were shaped by the collective wisdom of the group.

### 5. Co-develop the ARTEP Prep Plan

Armed with the insights from the interviews, Samad invited the soldiers to help co-develop the detailed training plan. This step underscores the OE principle that people support what they help create. By involving the team, the plan was improved, and the process also strengthened the soldiers' commitment to its success.

### 6. Implement and Improve the Plan

As they began implementing the plan, they held regular lessons-learned sessions, allowing for real-time adjustments and improvements. This iterative process, which emphasized flexibility and responsiveness, was key to their approach. The entire process plan evolved organically.

### Result: Nail the ARTEP

The culmination of their efforts envisioned the successful completion of the ARTEP. This result symbolized the fulfillment of a shared mission.

As you reflect on the process graphic in figure 17.2, consider its relevance beyond the military context. This seven-step plan is more than just a relic of the past; it's a living example of how collaborative planning, continuous feedback, and adaptive execution can lead to success in any field today. Whether in business, education, or any kind of human endeavor, these principles hold the potential to transform challenges into triumphs.

## CLOSING THE LOOP

As the ARTEP approached, Jack felt a bittersweet mix of pride and regret as he prepared to leave for his OE deployment along the East German border. He hated not being with the battalion for the actual test, but he was confident that Samad and the team would do well. They'd become more than a team prepping for an ARTEP; they became a band of brothers, united by a shared mission and more.

Weeks later, Samad's voice over the phone carried the news Jack had hoped for: the battalion had passed the ARTEP with flying colors. They'd not only succeeded, they'd excelled, earning the commanding general's streamer for superior performance in the process.

"We nailed it, Jack," Samad said. "This wasn't just a win. It was proof of what people can achieve when they truly work together. Thanks for showing us the ropes!"

As Jack hung up the phone, he leaned back in his chair, savoring the moment. How remarkable it was that a few commonsense principles, the courage to try something different, and a lot of commitment and hard work could transform a challenge into an experience that felt, well, almost prehistoric.

# 18 Co-Creating with Others

People support what they help create.

—Anonymous

*Fort Lewis, Washington. During the ARTEP prep.*

Reflecting on his journey from being a young army officer in Vietnam to what he calls his "elderhood," Jack often considers how providential many of his life's experiences have been—how one led to another without much intervention on his part.

Few of those experiences stand out as vividly as his time at the army's OE school, and even fewer were accompanied by truisms so compelling they seemed to etch themselves into Jack's soul.

Truisms are statements so self-evident that they hardly need saying, such as "Actions speak louder than words," "What goes around comes around," and "You can't please everybody." These concise sayings simplify complex ideas, reinforce common beliefs, and create shared understanding. Occasionally, a single truth resonates so deeply that it can change your entire outlook on life.

One such truth struck a deep chord for Jack when he first heard it during the OE course: "People support what they help create." Like a key unlocking a door, its wisdom clarified a reality he'd sensed for a long time but had never put into words. When people truly collaborate, their relationships deepen, trust grows, and those bonds become stepping stones to higher performance.

Turning this insight over in his mind, Jack began to see his career through a new lens. His past successes and failures boiled down to the presence or absence of real collaboration. The challenge now was how to turn this awareness into action. He didn't have to wait long.

## TURNING INSIGHT INTO ACTION

You've seen how, soon after completing his OE training, Jack got the perfect chance to put his insight about collaboration to the test. His good friend and army buddy Egan Samad asked him to help prepare his artillery unit for their annual operational proficiency evaluation, the ARTEP. What followed became a watershed moment in Jack's development as a leader.

Working alongside Samad throughout the preparations for the ARTEP, Jack witnessed the transformative power of involving people and encouraging them to actively participate in achieving a common goal. Jack joined planning meetings, engaged with soldiers, listened closely, and exchanged ideas about how to best tackle ARTEP tasks. He noticed how freely Samad's soldiers contributed their unique insights and energy to the mission.

One evening, during a nightly after-action review, Sergeant First Class Fulkerson, the senior enlisted man on the team, approached Samad and Jack to offer feedback on the preparations. Addressing them both, he began, "Sirs, I'd like to give you some feedback about the preparations we've been going through. I've been in the army for a lot of years, and what we're doing here—and how we're doing it—is, well, *different*."

"Please go on, Sergeant." Samad encouraged.

"It's the way we're all working together. How the two of you and Lieutenant Kirk are always around, alongside of us, how you have your sleeves rolled up, helping—not bossing us. We haven't worked with any of you before. Captain Samad, you and Lieutenant Kirk just joined us in Operations."

Making eye contact with Jack, Fulkerson continued. "And Captain Barrett, we know you're here helping temporarily, and we appreciate it. Thank you."

Pausing as if carefully weighing what he wanted to say next, Fulkerson said, "No disrespect, but the men and I have talked about this. We know you're officers and we appreciate that, but in this work we're doing, it feels almost as if we're all 'equal.' None of us have ever been in a situation like this before. Like I said, what's going here on is different. I wish I had more words to describe it."

Reflecting the thought behind Fulkerson's words, Jack responded, "So it sounds like you're saying that you and the others think what's going on is positive. Do I have that right?"

"Yes, sir. Very much so. I'll speak for myself. This is the first time I've ever been genuinely involved—the first time my opinion has truly been solicited and considered—and the first time in my career work hasn't just been about following orders. I feel like a part of a real team working toward an important shared goal, and I know the others feel the same way. This is what I've always believed teamwork should be."

The sergeant's sincerity left a deep impression on both Egan and Jack. For Samad, it was the encouragement and the vote of confidence he needed to actually start settling into his new job and give it everything he had. The timing couldn't have been better.

For Jack, Fulkerson reinforced his belief in the positive impact that OE could have in the army. Helping Samad and his soldiers prepare for the ARTEP didn't just give Jack a sense of professional fulfillment, it revitalized his belief in the power of teamwork. The soldiers' cohesion and can-do spirit reminded him of some of his own experiences working with his team in Vietnam.

Jack was elated by witnessing the power of the simple idea that people support what they help create in a peacetime army. It made him a true believer. From that moment on, he promised himself that in whatever work he did in the future, he'd be guided by what he'd learned about working together from Samad and his soldiers.

## THE EVOLUTION OF WORKING TOGETHER

What Jack learned and applied as a leadership tool in the army—the idea that people support what they help create—has since evolved into a powerful business practice in the commercial world. Today, the same things Jack witnessed in action during Samad's ARTEP prep, such as the power of shared purpose, collaboration, and mutual investment in success are the heart of a widely recognized product and service development strategy known as *business co-creation*.

Companies using this strategy invite customers to work together with company employees—typically marketing or product development professionals—to come up with new products or services or to improve existing ones. Business co-creation gained momentum in the late twentieth and early twenty-first centuries and has since become one of the most successful business practices ever adapted from the behavioral sciences.

Today, many companies assert that business co-creation is the pinnacle of collaboration—the summit of working together. But is it really? We'll examine this closely as this chapter proceeds.

## THE HISTORICAL ROOTS OF BUSINESS CO-CREATION

The instinct to cooperate runs deep in human history. From Mesopotamian communities joining forces on agriculture and flood control projects to early hominin groups crafting tools, collective effort is woven into the fabric of who we are.

As Victor Udoewa from NASA puts it in his presentation "The Origins of Participatory Design," collaboration has always been at the core of our survival and progress as a species."[1]

Another example of this innate human behavior can be found in the principle "The customer is always right," introduced by American retailer Harry Gordon Selfridge at the turn of the last century at his iconic department store on Oxford Street in London.[2]

Selfridge revolutionized the way his employees engaged with the public by charging them to embrace this principle. This marked the beginning of a shift from transactional to relationship-based business models built on cooperation and mutual respect that still exist in many companies today.

While Selfridge's idea was radical in its time, it has evolved today into something even more powerful: a model of engagement where businesses and customers collaborate closely. Together, they co-create products and services that reflect the needs and desires of the people who use them.

Throughout history, cooperation has driven human achievements—from curing diseases to advancing civil rights, from exploring space to rebuilding after wars.

Working together to achieve common goals and the shift toward collaboration and co-creation isn't just a trend. It reflects a deeper truth about human nature. Humanity's adaptive spirit and enduring resilience have always underpinned our most significant achievements.

## CO-CREATION IN THE BUSINESS WORLD TODAY

From ancient societies to the modern business world, history provides compelling evidence that humanity's greatest accomplishments occur when we harmonize what we do with who we are as people.

In the modern era, our innate instinct to work together has evolved from a survival mechanism into a cornerstone of business philosophy.

No longer are customers seen as passive buyers; today, they are active partners in helping shape the products and services they consume.

In the 1990s and early 2000s, a few pioneering companies, fueled by advances in technology and heightened marketplace competition, began to appreciate the potential of engaging more deeply with their customers. They've never looked back.

Thanks to thought leaders like the late C. K. Prahalad and Venkat Ramaswamy, the concept of co-creation—where customers become contributors rather than consumers—began to take hold.[3]

Today, platforms such as LEGO Ideas, My Starbucks Idea, Nike By You, and BMW's Co-Creation Lab invite customers into the design and development process, improving product quality while fostering passionate communities of brand advocates who provide feedback, suggest improvements, and even beta test new products.[4]

This evolution has fundamentally transformed company-customer relationships, though we're still in the early stages of this shift. As we move into the second quarter of the twenty-first century, advances in digital technology—particularly artificial intelligence—are accelerating the adoption of co-creation. Consider these findings from a 2023 survey of 554 senior executives and directors across European business sectors:

- 57 percent reported that co-creation has transformed their company's approach to innovation.
- 52 percent said adopting co-creation has reduced the costs of developing products and services.
- 51 percent indicated that co-creation has improved their company's financial performance.[5]

These statistics reveal co-creation's profound impact on the corporate landscape, suggesting we may be entering a new era of business innovation. However, many leaders are still holding back.

## TWO FRIENDS

A few years ago, two friends were gambling at a craps table in North Lake Tahoe, Nevada. Amid the ups and downs of the game, one moment stood out: they both placed the same wager on the same number and won several thousand dollars each. In the middle of the celebration, one turned to the other and said, with unexpected seriousness, "We're not bettin' enough, brother!"

The thrill of the friends' good luck is undeniable, but it also reveals something more: success often prompts the question "What if?" Could they have achieved more by betting bigger? Or did things work out positively because they took just the right risk at the right time?

As a leader, you face similar what-ifs every day. Like the friends gambling at the craps table, it's up to you to decide how much to risk. You know that leadership isn't about blind bets. It's about making the right call with the right people. The question isn't just whether to take risks but how you take them and who you take them with.

Elliott Jaques and Stephen D. Clement begin to frame the answer by describing leadership as "the process of getting others to move along with you—and each other—with competence and full commitment toward a shared goal."[6]

How your particular leadership process unfolds—whether through authoritarian or co-creative means—ultimately determines the level of your team's enrollment and success.

Consider Jaques and Clement's definition. An authoritarian approach may be successful in enforcing compliance, but it will rarely foster an environment in which people will willingly show and use their competence and full commitment. In contrast, a collaborative approach is far more likely to inspire and unite a team, leading to higher levels of engagement and performance.

It seems self-evident. Real leadership isn't about titles or authority but about trust, commitment, and the strength of those around you.

One of the places where this is most clear is in the world of mountaineering, where collaboration isn't just a philosophy, it's a matter of survival.

## MAKING A PUSH FOR THE TOP OF THE MOUNTAIN

We once worked briefly with a team of accomplished mountain climbers, men and women who lived by an unwritten code they called the "Brother and Sisterhood of the Rope."[7] They understood that when they were on the mountain, they were linked together as one by how well they worked together as surely as they were by the strength of their climbing ropes and carabiners. Collaboration was the lifeline that connected them on every ascent.

In mountaineering, as in real leadership, it's not about forcing others up the mountain; it's about moving together, securing each other's footing, and knowing that the strength of the team determines whether you reach the top.

In every leadership moment, you're faced with a choice: demand compliance and hope for the best or foster commitment and climb higher together than you ever could alone. The best leaders don't pull from above or push from below; they climb alongside, encouraging everyone along the way.

## CROSSROADS

We included these two stories—the one about the two friends gambling and the mountaineers—to illustrate an abiding truth about leadership: every day, moment by moment, decision by decision, we stand at a crossroads. Do we make a bold leap toward the summit or retreat to the relative comfort of base camp?

Our choices don't just shape the present; they have lasting consequences for our professional standing as leaders. At its core, leadership is a profession of influence—yours and ours—which is why we need to wield that influence with purpose and integrity.

We understand that betting big on co-creation can feel risky. But in reality, going all in is often the safer choice. Your leadership determines whether people bring their full competence and commitment to their work—and whether they channel those strengths toward a shared goal.

The ability to choose how you lead gives you extraordinary latitude to shape the factor most critical to your team's success: their willingness to offer discretionary commitment and energy to the purpose and goals you share. Given that you do have this choice, doesn't it deserve your careful attention?

Before you answer, consider this: how much more innovative, effective, and fulfilled could your team be if you unlocked their hidden reserves of energy, creativity, and dedication? Or ask yourself an even more revealing question: what would it take for your boss to unlock yours?

Like the two friends at Lake Tahoe, isn't it time to make bigger bets on ourselves and our teams? And like our friends the mountain climbers, isn't it time to push for the true summit of leadership to embrace collaboration as if our lives and livelihoods depended on it? We say, unreservedly, yes!

## THE REAL SUMMIT OF COLLABORATIVE LEADERSHIP: TEAM CO-CREATION

Earlier, we challenged the notion that business co-creation is the ultimate form of collaboration. We thought so once, but our perspective has evolved. Just as a seasoned climber knows that not every distant peak is the highest, we realized that while business co-creation yields impressive results, it's not the pinnacle of collaborative leadership. The true summit lies within the emerging practice of *team co-creation.*

Team co-creation happens when individuals—each operating with the creative autonomy born of their personal agency—deliberately come together to achieve something greater than any one of them could accomplish alone. It's about solving problems collectively, generating new ideas, and overcoming obstacles to reach shared goals.

At its core, this reflects the definition of leadership we've used throughout this book, taken from Jaques and Clement: "Leadership is the process of getting others to move along with you—and each other—with competence and full commitment toward a shared goal."[8]

Team co-creation is the embodiment of this definition, where the shared goal becomes the focal point for collective effort.

Dig a little deeper, and you'll find that team co-creation shares a key characteristic with the unconventional principle that made Will Guidara's Manhattan restaurant Eleven Madison Park the number-one restaurant in the world in 2017: being unreasonable.

Yes, you read that correctly: being unreasonable.

In his *New York Times* best-selling book *Unreasonable Hospitality*, and in many of his public appearances, Guidara emphasizes that hospitality is about making people "feel seen."[9] His choice of words—*feel seen*—is important.

Guidara's philosophy of unreasonableness underscores another key point: success isn't just about meeting standards. It's about doing something extraordinary that leaves a lasting impact. The real genius of Eleven Madison Park wasn't just about the guests feeling seen; it was Guidara's insight that for this to happen, he first needed to ensure his team felt seen.

This is the same idea, expressed differently, that Jack and Egan recognized before preparing for the ARTEP. They agreed that success depended on paying attention to soldiers and involving them in meaningful ways. Samad captured this powerfully with his equally straightforward declaration, "Hot damn, Jack! It's not rocket science, is it?"

No, it wasn't then. It still isn't now. And it won't be tomorrow.

The leadership approach this book espouses is closely akin to Guidara's concept of hospitality. Success rests on people feeling seen. And in leadership, two of the best ways to ensure the people you work with feel seen are to give them your attention and involve them in your plans. These steps are the precursors to becoming a co-creative team.

What if you challenged yourself and your team to be unreasonable in how you work together? Imagine a project where everyone's expertise, energy, and creativity are fully engaged. The demands would be high and the intensity palpable, but the rewards—unparalleled results and a thriving team culture—would be priceless.

Few leadership actions carry the truly transformative power of embracing an approach based on team co-creation. Co-creation embodies every aspect of the Leadership Actually Model—mindset, skilled leadership knowledge, and personal sensibilities—all working in harmony to achieve exceptional results while strengthening team cohesion and ensuring long-term success.

Understanding the power of co-creating with others is one thing; actually doing it is another. The good news? You can develop this skilled knowledge one step at a time. How do you begin fostering this dynamic within your own team? Here are some proven ideas for how to get started.

## TIPS FOR GETTING STARTED WITH TEAM CO-CREATION

Embarking on the journey toward team co-creation doesn't require a giant leap; rather, it starts with small, deliberate steps. Like almost everything in leadership, co-creating with others demands determination, consistent practice, and a willingness to experiment—even if that means making mistakes along the way.

By gradually introducing your team to co-creation and applying the leadership mindset, skilled leadership knowledge, and personal sensibilities outlined in the Leadership Actually Model, you'll be planting the seeds for future success.

Here are some practical ways to begin making co-creation a reality with your team:

- Adopt co-creation as a team challenge for the next six to twelve months, using chapters 15 and 16 as a guide.
- Develop a streamlined communications plan to introduce co-creation using the SHARE model (see chapters 11 and 12).
- Be transparent about your approach. Describe what you've learned, explain why you want to try co-creation, and invite your team into the process.
- Provide shared learning resources. Consider giving each team member a copy of this book and hosting short workshops on key concepts, starting with the three pillars of leadership (see chapters 1 and 2).
- Work with team members to develop a co-creative training plan focused on developing knowledge and practical leadership skills (see parts 2 and 3).
- Involve team members in co-facilitating regular team learning sessions. Use the process questions from chapter 8 to deepen everyone's understanding:
    - "What happened?"
    - "Who was involved?"
    - "How am I reacting?"
    - "What's the lesson from this?"
- Act together. When your team is ready, identify a challenge you keep putting on the back burner—one you know can be solved.

- Share it with your team and invite them to tackle it with you *co-creatively*. Two heads are better than one.

Embracing a developmental and co-creative approach like this isn't just about improving your team's effectiveness. It's about refining your own leadership in real time. Every step you take is tied to the Leadership Actually Model in a practical way, strengthening both your team and your personal growth as a leader.

## BRINGING IT ALL TOGETHER

Co-creating with others is the culmination of the skilled leadership knowledge presented in this book. When you use it effectively, you'll employ every bit of what we've covered here, including the following:

- Recognizing and addressing the crucial differences between the illusion of leading and how it's actually done, embracing agency over empowerment, awareness over obliviousness, and commitment over compliance (chapter 2)
- Adopting the Jaques and Clement definition of what leadership is truly all about regardless of the approach you may use (chapter 2)
- Understanding that the three pillars of leadership are always present whether or not you are attentive to and fully employ them (chapter 2)
- Acknowledging the criticality of moving beyond dependent to cooperative, collaborative, and then interdependent working relationships and how promoting people's personal agency fits in (chapter 4)
- Fully embracing the new twenty-first century leadership imperative that you treat your work like the craft it surely is (chapter 6)
- Being hyperaware of the impact content and process have on every interaction you have with others (chapter 8)

- Knowing that the more self-aware you become, the more effective you become in working and living with others (chapter 10)
- Using the knowledge of how to turn information into communication to positively impact everyone in your life (chapter 12)
- Appreciating the all-important necessity of managing team process (chapter 14)
- Employing the most powerful tool at your disposal for unlocking the full current and future potential of your team—teaching and learning together with them (chapter 16).

When you co-create with your team, you embody everything on this list and more, and even so, you're only at the beginning of your leadership journey as you continue to become the leader you are meant to be. As you put these ideas into practice, you'll start to see your work as a place where challenges, working relationships, and opportunities intersect. Remember what we said in the first ten pages of this book:

You are needed.
Your leadership matters.
Nothing changes if nothing changes.
Start small.
Start now.

## EXTRAS: CHAPTERS 17 AND 18

### Chapters 17 and 18 Summary

- Faced with a thirty-day gap between completing the OE course and reporting to his new duty station near the East German border, Jack devised a plan to avoid wasting a full month while simultaneously helping his friend Captain Egan Samad prepare for the upcoming ARTEP.

- As his unit's new operations officer, Samad was responsible for ensuring his artillery battalion passed the annual ARTEP after two consecutive failures.
- Samad asked Jack to help him improve his team's performance on the ARTEP by applying what he'd learned at the OE school. They agreed to base their joint work on two key OE principles: "People support what they help create." "The classroom isn't a place; it's a mindset."
- Jack and Samad devised a seven-step process plan called "Nail the ARTEP," which focused on collaborating, giving and getting real-time feedback, and engaging soldiers in the process.
- Although Jack left for his next duty station in Germany before the ARTEP began, the battalion passed with superior results, earning recognition from the commanding general.
- When Jack reflected on his life experiences, particularly his time at the Army's Organizational Effectiveness (OE) school, he discovered how profoundly he'd been influenced by the principle "People support what they help create."
- Jack's experience helping Samad with ARTEP preparations showed the power of involving people in decision-making and teamwork. Soldiers felt more engaged and committed when their opinions were valued.
- This experience reaffirmed Jack's belief in teamwork and the positive effects of collaboration that mirrored his time in Vietnam, where teamwork was essential for survival.
- The concept of co-creation, where customers collaborate with companies, has evolved into a powerful business strategy.
- Pioneers like C. K. Prahalad and Venkat Ramaswamy popularized this approach, leading to customer-driven innovation and improved company performance.
- Today, platforms like LEGO Ideas, My Starbucks Idea, and BMW's Co-Creation Lab show how businesses engage

customers to co-create products and services, driving innovation and fostering brand loyalty.

- A 2023 survey in Europe found that co-creation has transformed business innovation, reduced product development costs, and improved financial performance for companies who adopted the strategy.
- While business co-creation is powerful, team co-creation—where a group works together to achieve greater results than they could individually—represents the pinnacle of collaborative leadership.
- Team co-creation involves collective problem-solving and idea generation, where everyone contributes fully, akin to the unreasonable commitment seen in the success of Will Guidara's Eleven Madison Park restaurant.
- Co-creating with others is the culmination of the skilled leadership knowledge presented in this book.

## How to Use the Information in Chapters 17 and 18

As you look back over Jack's story, take a moment to reflect on the principles that have shaped your journey. Which ones have most influenced your life and work, and what surprises you about their lasting impact?

Think back to a time when you were fully committed to a project. What leadership style was in place? How did it affect your engagement and the outcome?

Verse 12, *Tao Te Ching*

An excess of light blinds the human eye;
an excess of noise ruins the ear;
an excess of condiments deadens the taste.

The effect of too much horse racing and hunting is bad,
and the lure of hidden treasure tempts one to do evil.
Therefore the wise man attends to the inner significance of things
and does not concern himself with outward appearances.
Therefore he ignores matter and seeks the spirit.

## Final Thoughts

We've poured our best thinking, energy, and heart into writing a book we hope makes a difference for you. Still, it comes back to the simple truth: "Nothing changes if nothing changes." The next move is yours.

We're here, ready and eager to hear from you. As you consider the next steps you'll take in your leadership journey, we sincerely wish you Godspeed.

# Epilogue
# Here Comes the Sun

On the last day of the world,
I would want to plant a tree.
—W. S. Merwin

*The Southwestern United States. Autumn 2021.*

Returning from a walk with his Australian Labradoodle, Tilly, Jack was surprised to find a small package on his doorstep. He hadn't been expecting anything, certainly not something that would stop him in his tracks and carry him back fifty years to a time when he was young, filled with restless energy, and dreamed about how he would make the world a better, more peaceful place.

The package was from Loni Drexler, Gary's wife, who'd told him at Gary's memorial service six months earlier to expect something in the mail. Nothing had come, so Jack had forgotten about it until this moment.

Jack carried the box inside and set it gently on the kitchen table. Inside, he found a wrapped bundle topped with a note in Gary's familiar scrawl. "Jack, I've kept this all these years. It's yours again now. Pass it along when the time comes. Gary."

Jack's fingers brushed the paper. He was hesitant, worried that unwrapping it might make the moment feel too much like an ending. Beneath the delicate tissue lay the fragile stained-glass suncatcher he'd shaped into a peace symbol so many years ago. Its colors were still vivid, as if time had only deepened their glow.

As he held it, the glass warm in his palm, memories came flooding back. Jack felt Gary's presence and heard his voice urging him to keep seeking, questioning, leading, and teaching—always circling back to the hard-won truths he'd discovered.

Gary had been more than a teacher. He'd been a friend, a mentor, and a leader in the truest sense—someone who cared, listened deeply, and guided Jack and others to find their own paths.

Jack walked to the window by his breakfast table and hung the suncatcher up carefully. The room filled with a soft cascade of colors, casting vivid patterns across the walls. It was a final gift from Gary, a reminder of the circles they'd both walked and of the work that still lay ahead—the quiet labor of listening, teaching, and fostering the peace that Gary had modeled so well.

Jack stood quietly, letting the light settle around him, and whispered the words of an old hymn he remembered his father singing under his breath occasionally. "May the circle be unbroken, by and by, Lord, by and by. May the circle be unbroken . . ."

The melody wove its way through the circles of light now filling the room with its timeless message to celebrate enduring connections, shared hope, and the resilience of the human spirit. It was everything Gary lived for and everything that Jack vowed to carry forward.

# Afterword

Before we look ahead, we want to acknowledge an idea from the late professor and Catholic priest Ivan Illich—one that shaped both our thinking about change and our decision to write this book. "Neither revolution nor reformation can ultimately change a society; rather, you must tell a new, powerful tale—one so persuasive that it sweeps away old myths and becomes the preferred story, one so inclusive that it gathers all the bits of our past and present into a coherent whole, one that even shines some light into the future so that we can take the next step."[1]

We came across this insight unexpectedly—something that brought to mind a favorite line from Paulo Coelho's *The Zahir*: "All you have to do is pay attention; the lessons always arrive when you are ready."[2]

Illich's perspective challenged us to reconsider what leadership truly is, how it's practiced, and how it's cultivated. It led us to ask, What if leadership isn't just a role but a shared and evolving story? If stories have the power to reshape societies, surely they can transform leadership as well.

This belief is what underpins our work and this book, *Leadership Actually*, the first in a three-part series we call the Leadership Actually Trilogy. The next two volumes, *Inside the Three-Square Meters* and *Dispatches from the Frontlines of Leadership*, are in development and will continue the exploration of what leadership can and should mean today.

These books are not a traditional trilogy with a neat beginning, middle, and end. Rather, they are contributions to a larger ongoing conversation—one that we hope you'll join. With *Leadership Actually*, we've invited you to see leadership not as an illusion or status but instead as something deeply real, grounded in presence, care, and collaboration.

The story doesn't end here.

Now it's your turn. Take what you've read, test the ideas, share them, and challenge them. Bring your own questions to the conversation. Talk about them with your team, your mentors, your critics, and especially those you lead. Leadership isn't something we inherit; it's something we co-create, every day.

Let's keep writing this story—together.

# Acknowledgments

To all those who labor—quietly or boldly, visibly or unseen—to make leadership humane, generative, and real: you are the reason this work exists.

We are deeply grateful to all those who have accompanied us on the long crossing between who we were and who we are still becoming—a journey whose early stretches are retold in this book. This work would not exist without the encouragement, wisdom, and generosity of so many who shared their insights, challenged our assumptions, and supported us along the way. To borrow from the poet-troubadour Don Henley, this is our Thanksgiving—and it is with that spirit of gratitude that we turn to the people who shaped this work most directly.

We offer our gratitude to Dr. Randy White, whose sage guidance and warm welcome steadied us at the uncertain beginning of this writing journey; to Rob Meekins, whose steadfast advice and thoughtful insights—including his creative hand in shaping our logo—helped bring clarity and vision to our work; and to Sarah Cheney Redgrave, whose brilliance and incisive observations reminded us that leadership is always far more than the pursuit of a goal.

We thank Cathy Ruspino of Sydney, Australia, whose suggestion of "altocumulus clouds" in Jack Barrett's "Attention Must Be Paid" story strengthened our commitment to precision and accuracy in storytelling; E. R. Dunn for encouragement that has never once wavered; General David P. Fridovich for nearly fifty years of friendship and for thirty-seven years of leadership service to the nation and the world—DOL, Frido!; Chan Lai Huat and Felina Chua, dear friends and colleagues in Singapore, for their enduring friendship and for honoring us as the very first supporters of *Leadership Actually*; David "the Lone Ranger" Kinsman in Kunming, China, a source of strength, joy, and endless humor throughout this journey and a friend for life; and R. Thomas Lenz, Emeritus Professor of Business and Strategy at Indiana University, who is always ready to offer the best of what he has—and it is always terrific.

We are grateful to Jerry Eppler—visionary, pioneer of the US Army's Organizational Effectiveness School, and explorer of the human spirit—who taught us not only how to fish but how to teach others to do the same—and to Elliott Jaques, teacher, mentor, friend, and purveyor of countless gifts of knowledge, too many to list but none forgotten.

We thank Robert E. Quinn, Margaret Elliot Tracy Collegiate Professor Emeritus at the University of Michigan Ross School of Business—the first person we spoke to about writing this book—whose opening question, "Can you talk about your subject for eight hours?" set the tone for our journey. After countless hours, pages, and conversations, our answer today is "Yes, and then some."

We also thank General Robert W. Sennewald, a craftsman of leadership before there was even a name for such a calling; Colonel Paul A. McGowan, the kind of commanding officer any parents would want their child to serve with and learn from; Liem Tien Pao of Jakarta, Indonesia, who taught us the principle of "the good of the whole" and who continues to live it by example; and Gary Micheau, a real leader who always assured those who worked with him that they never need worry about whether he had their backs. We didn't—and, true to his word, he always followed through.

We offer thanks to John Scelfo, who taught us the value of building bridges instead of fences, and to J. E. (JED) Daniel, a true-to-life leader in every sense of the word. We're grateful to Kami Welsh for her invaluable market insights and unwavering support of our efforts both locally and beyond—she truly embodies the spirit of collaboration and co-creativity.

We thank Marco and Jane Angelini in London for their decades-long friendship, for their thoughtful comments on our manuscript, and especially for their guidance on the use of color on our cover—their discerning eye made the book stronger.

We thank Beth and Kellen Williams for their early help in bringing this book to life; Loni Tyrowski for her gentle spirit, friendship, and steadfast work for what is right; and Quang Do for his infectious enthusiasm and personal commitment to our endeavor, which has inspired us greatly.

We are grateful to Dan Bushell for recognizing and naming "our ministry" before we were aware of it ourselves and to Webb Bassick IV for enlivening that endeavor with the gift of his friendship. We thank our dear friend Nicole Bendig-Lamb for sharing her book-writing experience and cheering us on throughout our journey—her encouragement has meant the world to us.

We thank Jay Vineyard for teaching us what it means to "ride the tiger"; Bob Knerr for helping us learn how to ask for help when we need it; and Clinton Webb for his creativity and generous engagement with our website—we are truly fortunate to have him as part of our alliance.

We are indebted to Joan Smith and Ann Dahmer, who endured the endless and meandering early drafts of this book, and Sharon Goldinger of PeopleSpeak, whose professionalism and eye for details transformed our raw manuscript into a real book. We could not have done it without her.

We also could not have written *Leadership Actually* without the unflagging support and encouragement of our families, spouses, children, and yes, even grandchildren. Their love and steady presence have carried us through early mornings, long nights, and the many quiet in-between moments that made this work possible.

Finally, to all those whose names may not appear here but whose influence and friendship are deeply felt, we thank you. Your presence and support are woven into the very fabric of *Leadership Actually*. Each page carries the traces of your wisdom, humor, and love. To all of you, we remain forever grateful.

# Appendix A
# The Listening Ladder: Five Techniques for You to Master

One of the keys to leading effectively is your ability to listen deeply, intentionally, and without rushing to respond. The "Listening Ladder" is a framework that outlines five essential techniques you can use to improve your listening skills, moving from foundational to more advanced practices.

## 1. SILENCE

You might be surprised that silence is included as a listening skill. The fact is that silence is the bedrock of effective listening. By resisting the urge to interrupt, comment, or formulate your own response while the other person is speaking and instead remain quiet, you can create space for deeper dialogue. Silence signals respect, allows for reflection, and encourages the speaker to share more fully.

## 2. NEUTRAL RESPONSES

Neutral responses—such as nodding or saying, "I see"—communicate presence and attentiveness without inserting judgment or direction. These responses acknowledge the speaker's words without steering the conversation prematurely, allowing them to express themselves fully. Here are a few more responses that fit into this category:

- "Oh."
- "Mmm."
- "Interesting."
- "Got it."
- "I understand."
- "Uh-huh."
- "I hear you."
- "Heard."
- "Noted."
- "I'm listening."

These responses are simple and neutral ways to show another person you're engaged in the conversation without adding any judgment. The main point is that they keep the communication channel open.

## 3. INVITATIONS TO SAY MORE

Encouraging someone to elaborate fosters clarity and depth. Simple prompts such as "Please tell me more about that" or "I'd enjoy hearing the rest of your perspective on this" signal genuine interest and help uncover underlying thoughts, emotions, and concerns that might not surface otherwise. Here's a list of neutral, open-ended invitations you can use to encourage someone to say more:

- "Please elaborate."
- "Go on."
- "I'd love to hear more."
- "I can tell there's more to this."
- "Please continue. This is interesting."
- "You've got my attention. Keep going."

## 4. PARAPHRASING

Restating what the speaker has said in your own words demonstrates comprehension and provides an opportunity for clarification. For example, you could say, "So what I'm hearing is that you're concerned about the deadline. Do I have that right?" This ensures alignment and builds trust.

## 5. REFLECTIVE LISTENING

The highest level of listening involves not just repeating the content but also acknowledging any underlying emotions and implications. A reflective response might sound like "It sounds like you're feeling frustrated because you don't have the resources you need to meet expectations. Does that capture it?" This deepens the conversation and fosters meaningful connection.

By climbing the listening ladder, you can cultivate stronger relationships, foster a culture of trust, and make better-informed decisions. Mastering these five techniques transforms listening from a passive act into a powerful tool for leading actually.

# Appendix B
# Have To/Choose To (HT/CT): A Self-Awareness Activity

The "Have To/Choose To" (HT/CT) activity is one of our favorite self-awareness exercises because it has the power to flip critical mental switches that may have been turned off over time, often without our realizing it. HT/CT helps turn them back on.

Have you ever felt like life is just happening to you, as if your choices have already been made before you even get a say? Many people today seem to have lost their sense of personal agency—the freedom to act autonomously to make meaningful decisions that shape their outcomes—not because they lack the ability to choose but because they've been conditioned to believe their choices don't matter. Over time, the weight of obligations, expectations, and pressures can create the illusion that we're all merely following a script rather than actively shaping our lives.

This erosion of agency isn't accidental. It's often the byproduct of modern life—unrelenting pressures, constant deadlines, and ever-rising expectations. Add to these the widespread and deeply ingrained habits of command-and-control leadership—at work, in institutions, and even in cultural norms—and the result is an environment that fosters the illusion that decisions are made for us rather than by us.

Making matters worse, this degradation in the ability to choose freely is a double-edged sword. Because choice is deeply connected to creativity, when people lose sight of their agency, they also lose the confidence to think beyond the expected, challenge assumptions, take risks, and imagine new possibilities.

A striking example of how conditioning suppresses independent thinking comes from a well-known longitudinal study conducted by Dr. George Land for NASA to assess creativity in children.[1] The study tracked sixteen hundred children over time, measuring their ability to think creatively, and found these results:

- At age five, 98 percent of the children scored at a "creative genius" level.
- By age ten, that number had dropped to 30 percent.
- By age fifteen, it had fallen further to 12 percent.
- By adulthood, only 2 percent retained their ability to think at a creative genius level.

Land's conclusion was that traditional schooling and societal structures don't just suppress agency and creativity. They train people to doubt their own ideas, wait for permission, ask to be empowered, or default to external expectations rather than their own initiative.

## RECLAIMING YOUR AGENCY

The good news is that once we recognize this pattern, we can break it. The ability to choose—intentionally, mindfully, and creatively—lies within us. The key is to find its On switch and flip it back on. HT/CT can help.

You can either engage in this activity alone or with another person you trust. The exercise is easy and nonthreatening and can illuminate the hidden consequences of how you talk to yourself. Jack participated in HT/CT during week one of the army's OE course, and he swears doing so was like moving through a portal to a new plane of understanding. HT/CT is as relevant to you today as it was for Jack, maybe more so. Here are the instructions.

### Round 1: "I Have To" Becomes "I Choose To"

In the first round, the goal is to switch from saying "I have to" to "I choose to."

1. Pair up and sit facing each other. Maintain eye contact.
2. Take turns saying sentences that begin with "I have to." List tasks you believe you *have* to do. Take about five minutes.
3. Go back and replace "I have to" with "I choose to." Say the sentences again, even if your choice is between two undesirable alternatives.
4. Reflect on how it feels to say "I choose to." Does your perspective shift? Add any follow-up sentences that naturally come to mind.
5. If you're doing HT/CT with a partner, discuss your experiences using the process questions we introduced in chapter 8:
   - What happened?
   - How did you react?
   - What did you learn?

### Round 2: "I Can't" Becomes "I Choose Not To"

In the second round, the power of choice gets amplified.

1. Take turns stating sentences that begin with "I can't." Make a list of things you believe you *cannot* do. Take about five minutes.
2. Replace "I can't" with "I choose not to," and say the sentences again.

3. Pay attention to how this change feels. Is this something truly impossible or something you refuse to do?
4. Discuss:
   - How did it feel to take responsibility for your refusal?
   - What insights did you gain?

## Round 3: "I Need" Becomes "I Want"

In the third round, the difference between needs and wants gets clarified.

1. Take turns stating sentences that begin with "I need." Make a list of things you believe you *need*. Take about five minutes.
2. Replace "I need " with "I want," and say the sentences again.
3. Reflect on whether these items are truly necessities or simply strong desires.
4. Discuss:
   - Did this exercise clarify the difference between needs and wants?
   - How might this awareness impact your choices?

## Round 4: "I'm Afraid To" Becomes "I'd Like To"

In the final round, fears get challenged and redefined.

1. Take turns stating sentences that begin with "I'm afraid to." Make a list of things you are afraid to try. Take about five minutes.
2. Now, replace "I'm afraid to" with "I'd like to," and say the sentences again.
3. Reflect on what attracts you to these risks. What might you gain?

4. Discuss:
   - How did changing your wording affect your perspective on fear?
   - Did this exercise help you see fear as a part of growth?

## CONSEQUENCES OF YOUR SELF-TALK

When your self-talk is full of "I have to," "I can't," "I need," or "I'm afraid to," you unknowingly diminish your own power. These phrases reinforce other negative states:

- Saying "I have to . . ." leads to feelings of obligation and resentment.
- Saying "I can't" and "I'm afraid to" leads to feelings of weakness or impotence.
- Saying "I need" leads to feelings of dependency and helplessness.

On the other hand, adopting "I choose to," "I choose not to," "I want," and "I'd like to" affirms your control over your life. Even if your choices remain the same, the shift in language reinforces your strength:

- Saying "I choose to" leads to an awareness of your power to act.
- Saying "I choose not to" leads to the ability to say no intentionally.
- Saying "I want" leads to the ability to distinguish between needs and desires.
- Saying "I'd like to" leads to the ability to recognize the balance of fear and possibility.

Every time you acknowledge your power to choose, you reinforce your personal agency—and that changes everything.

What small shift in the way to talk to yourself can you make today to help you reclaim your agency?

## THE REST OF JACK'S HT/CT STORY

### *US Army Organizational Effectiveness School, 1976.*

OE students were asked to make individual lists of the things they had to do daily. The first item on Jack's was "run" because it was the task he had to do that he hated most. It was also the one over which he felt he had the least control. Daily multimile runs were the army's go-to method for staying physically fit. So Jack was out on the road every afternoon or evening, trudging away and hating it every step of the way.

Doing HT/CT, Jack learned that what he really hated about running was the feeling of having little or no say about how he maintained his physical fitness. He had to run because the army required it.

Jack learned that by substituting "choose to" for "have to," he shifted the locus of control from the army to him, allowing him to understand that he ran because it was good for him, not because the army told him to. Not only did his mindset shift, but he eventually started enjoying running—so much so that he trained for and ran a marathon.

Appendix C

# Developing a Communication Plan

A communication plan provides a structured framework for delivering information effectively, ensuring your message resonates with your team rather than simply relaying facts and leaving people to interpret them on their own.

For instance, when announcing significant changes—such as reorganizations, new production processes, or leadership transitions—a well-designed communication plan helps you deliver messages in alignment with the SHARE process (signal, highlight, align, rally, execute). It also helps you avoid overlooking key audiences or missing critical details.

## USING THE 5W1H FRAMEWORK

One of the most effective ways to structure a communication plan is to use the 5W1H (who, what, when, where, why, and how) questioning technique. This approach ensures all essential aspects of communication are addressed:

- *Who*—Target audiences and stakeholders
- *What*—Key messages and content

- *When*—Timing and frequency
- *Where* —Communication channels
- *Why*—Purpose and desired outcomes
- *How*—Methods, tone, and execution

By structuring your plan around these elements, you ensure that communication is intentional, clear, and action-oriented rather than left to chance. See table A.1 for an example communication plan.

**TABLE A.1. EXAMPLE COMMUNICATION PLAN FRAMEWORK**

| Stage | Who | What | When | Where | Why | How |
|---|---|---|---|---|---|---|
| Signal | | | | | | |
| Highlight | | | | | | |
| Align | | | | | | |
| Rally | | | | | | |
| Execute | | | | | | |

# Appendix D
# Icebreakers

Icebreakers are short, interactive activities designed to warm up a group, encourage engagement, and create a sense of connection among participants. They help break down initial barriers, foster trust, and set a positive tone for discussions.

Whether you use them in team meetings, training sessions, or workshops, icebreakers serve as a powerful tool to create an open, collaborative environment. When thoughtfully chosen, they can make the interactions in your team more meaningful and pave the way for deeper conversations and stronger working relationships.

Here are five examples of quick and engaging icebreakers we like and use. Although they take less than twenty minutes, they still get the job done.

## 1. SPEED CONNECTING (10 TO 15 MINUTES)

Think of this as speed networking with a relational twist. Pair participants and give them two minutes each to answer these or other prompts:

- What were the highlights of your weekend?
- What's a small act of kindness someone did for you during the last week? How did you pay it forward?
- When did you last tell someone they did a good job?

After four minutes, have them rotate to a new partner. Do three to four rounds.

## 2. COMMON GROUND CHALLENGE (10 MINUTES)

Divide participants into small groups of three or four people. Give them three minutes to find five things they all have in common, work-related or personal. Obvious answers such as "We all work here" don't count.

Ask each group to share their discoveries aloud.

## 3. ONE-WORD CHECK-IN (5 TO 7 MINUTES)

Ask each person to share one word that describes how they interact in relationships (e.g., "listener," "connector," "curious"), then briefly explain their choice, allowing fifteen to twenty seconds per person. Words cannot be repeated.

## 4. THE COMPLIMENT CHAIN (10 TO 12 MINUTES)

Go around the group and ask each person to give a genuine, work-appropriate compliment to the person on their right (e.g., "You have a great energy that makes people feel comfortable"). That person then does the same with the person on their right, continuing until the last person compliments the first. This fosters warmth and positive interaction.

## 5. SILENT LINEUP (8 TO 10 MINUTES)

Challenge the group to line up in order based on a personal trait—without speaking. Here are some examples:

- By birth month
- By number of siblings
- By years in their current professional role

Once everyone is lined up, permit them to talk to confirm their order and briefly share something related to the topic.

If you'd like to dig deeper into icebreakers, here are two excellent references:

- *The Big Book of Icebreakers: Quick, Fun Activities for Energizing Meetings and Workshops* by Edie West.[1] This book offers a wide variety of icebreaker activities tailored to different types of groups, whether they're large or small, in-person or virtual. The activities are designed to help your team members get comfortable, build rapport, and set the stage for more effective collaboration.
- *The Ultimate Icebreaker Playbook: 30 Engaging Games, for Corporate, Classroom, Family, and Social Gatherings* by Omagamo.[2] This book includes a wide range of dynamic, easy-to-run icebreaker games designed to get people involved quickly.

## Appendix E

# Interviews before Training, Meetings, or Events

One-to-one interviews before an event are a valuable tool for gathering insights, shaping expectations, and generating anticipation within an organization. By engaging participants before an event, you can better understand what they've already heard about it, gain an understanding of what they hope to achieve, and learn about any concerns they may have. These interviews have the effect of starting the meeting before the meeting.

Additionally, these interviews can provide early feedback to help you fine-tune the event's focus and design. By capturing key themes—such as what excites people, what they're looking forward to, or what they hope to avoid—you can create an internal buzz that increases engagement and encourages broader participation.

Beyond gathering input, these interviews can help build momentum and create a sense of inclusion, signaling to participants that their voices matter. Ultimately, they also help ensure that the event will resonate with attendees, making it a more meaningful and valuable experience for everyone.

Here are some examples of the kinds of questions you can use for your interviews to help you gather input, identify expectations, and generate buzz within your organization:

- General awareness and perception:
  - What have you heard about the upcoming [event/meeting]?
  - How did you first learn about it?
  - What are people saying about it in your circles?
- Expectations and interests:
  - What do you hope to gain or achieve from this event?
  - Are there any specific topics or discussions you're particularly looking forward to?
  - If this event is a success, what will it look like for you?
- Concerns and potential barriers:
  - Is there anything you're unsure of or skeptical about regarding this event?
  - What would make this event or meeting feel like a waste of your time?
  - Are there any challenges or concerns that might prevent you from fully engaging?
- Engagement and excitement:
  - Based on what you know, if you were telling a colleague why they should attend, what would you say?
  - What's one thing that would make this event memorable or valuable for you?
  - If you could ask the organizers one question before the event, what would it be?

Following your interviews, you'll want to aggregate and analyze the information you collected. Sift through it together, identifying observations, themes, and, finally, findings.

If you use multiple interviewers, consider developing a written interview guide each of them can use during their conversations with people. A guide will help ensure that the resulting information will be easier to aggregate and analyze.

## THE OBSERVATIONS, THEMES, AND FINDINGS MODEL

If you want to go above and beyond and rack up some extra credit points from event participants after you've collected and aggregated the information you gleaned during your interviews, here is a never-fail approach we've used for years. It ensures that participants see their input reflected in the event, reinforcing engagement and signaling that their voices matter.

The Observations, Themes, and Findings Model provides a structured way to process and communicate insights before an event. Here's how it works.

### Step 1: Observations—Capturing the Raw Information of What You Heard

Observations are direct quotes, reactions, and notable comments gathered during pre-event interviews. At this stage, we simply record what was said—without filtering or analysis—to preserve authenticity.

- Guiding questions:
  - What are people saying about the event?
  - What questions, expectations, or concerns keep coming up?
  - What specific words, phrases, or sentiments are repeated?
- Example observations:
  - "I hope this event provides practical takeaways, not just discussions."
  - "People are unsure about the event's purpose. What's the big goal?"
  - "I've heard it's supposed to be interactive, but I'm not sure what that means."

## Step 2: Themes—Identifying Emerging Patterns and Grouping the Data

Themes emerge when you cluster similar observations into broad categories. These help you see when expectations are in alignment, diverge, or have potential gaps.

- Guiding questions:
  - What ideas, concerns, or expectations appear most frequently?
  - Are there clear areas of enthusiasm or hesitation?
  - Do responses suggest any misconceptions or misunderstandings?
- Example themes:
  - *Desire for practicality*—Participants want actionable insights, not just theory.
  - *Need for clarity*—Some attendees are unclear about the event's purpose.
  - *Engagement expectations*—People are anticipating an interactive, dynamic format.

## Step 3: Findings—Interpreting What the Data Says and Turning It into Insights and Actions

Findings transform themes into meaningful takeaways that can be addressed at the event. This step connects the insights gained during interviews to facilitation choices, agenda adjustments, or key messages.

- Guiding questions:
  - What do these themes tell you about participant expectations?
  - How can you incorporate this feedback into the event experience?
  - What do you need to communicate upfront to align expectations?

- Example findings and actions:
  - *Finding*—Many participants want hands-on, applicable content.
  - *Action*—Ensure the event includes interactive elements such as workshops or scenario discussions.
  - *Finding*—Some attendees don't fully grasp the event's objectives.
  - *Action*—Open the event with a clear, compelling statement of purpose and goals.
  - *Finding*—Excitement exists around the interactive format, but uncertainty remains.
  - *Action*—Provide a brief overview of what *interactive* means in this context and set expectations.

## Sharing Insights from the Interviews at the Event

At the start of the event, present a summary of key themes and findings. This helps participants feel heard and aligns expectations from the beginning. Some options for presenting this include the following:

- A short verbal summary during the event kickoff
- A slide with key themes and findings
- A handout or digital summary in the event materials
- A quick interactive poll asking attendees to react to or prioritize findings

## Why This Matters

By using the Observations, Themes, and Findings Model, you'll ensure that participant input informs the event experience, fostering a sense of shared ownership. This approach also helps event leaders anticipate potential concerns and proactively address them, creating a more engaging and valuable event for all involved.

# Notes

## PREFACE

1. All verses quoted in this book come from Lao Tzu, *Tao Te Ching*, trans. Dwight Goddard (London: John McMurray, 1919).

## CHAPTER 1

1. Jim Harter, "U.S. Employee Engagement Sinks to a 10-Year Low," Gallup, January 12, 2025, https://www.gallup.com/workplace/654911/employee-engagement-sinks-year-low.aspx.

## CHAPTER 2

1. Elliott Jaques and Stephen D. Clement, *Executive Leadership: A Practical Guide to Managing Complexity* (New York: Gordon and Breach Science, 1991), 4.

2. Talks at Google, Carol Dweck, "The Growth Mindset, Carol Dweck Talks at Google," March 2, 2007, YouTube video, 32:48, https://www.youtube.com/watch?v=-71zdXCMU6A.

3. John F. Kennedy, Inaugural Address 1961, National Archives, Milestone Documents, last reviewed February 8, 2022, https://www.archives.gov/milestone-documents/president-john-f-kennedys-inaugural-address.

4. *Merriam-Webster*, s.v. "attention," accessed March 6, 2024, https://www.merriam-webster.com/dictionary/attention.

5. Greater Good Science Center, "Jon Kabat-Zinn: What Is Mindfulness?" YouTube video, April 14, 2010, https://www.youtube.com/watch?v=xoLQ3qkh0w0.

6. *Merriam-Webster*, s.v. "commitment," accessed January 4, 2024, https://www.merriam-webster.com/dictionary/commitment.

7. Vocabulary.com, s.v. "communication." Accessed January 5, 2024, https://www.vocabulary.com/dictionary/communication.

8. Project Management Institute, "Project Management Professional," accessed February 5, 2024, https://www.pmi.org/certifications/project-management-pmp.

9. Rick Yvanovich, "Don't Feedback, Try Feedforward Instead!" TRG International, June 7, 2021.

10. Jaques and Clement, *Executive Leadership,* 4.

11. For more information about leadership mindsets, see Robert E. Quinn, "Moments of Greatness: Entering the Fundamental State of Leadership," *Harvard Business Review,* July–August 2005, https://hbr.org/2005/07/moments-of-greatness-entering-the-fundamental-state-of-leadership. Carol Dweck, "The Power of Believing That You Can Improve," TEDx, Norrkoping, Sweden, November 2014, https://www.ted.com/talks/carol_dweck_the_power_of_believing_that_you_can_improve; Tom Foster, "Who the Hell Is Elliott Jaques?," YouTube video, June 30, 2014, https:www.youtube.com/watch?v=RwRPTCbsXL8; and Jaques and Clement, *Executive Leadership.*

12. Robert E. Quinn, *Building the Bridge as You Walk on It: A Guide for Leading Change* (San Francisco: Jossey-Bass, 2004), 69–78.

## CHAPTER 3

1. Graham A. Cosmas, MACV: *The Joint Command in the Years of Withdrawal* (1968–1973)," The United States Army in Vietnam (Washington, DC: US Army, 2007), https://history.army.mil/html/books/091/91-7/CMH_Pub_91-7.pdf.

2. The World (always capitalized) referred to the United States. As in, "Where you from back in The World?" "Military Slang During the Vietnam

War," https://cherrieswriter.com/2014/02/13/military-speak-during-the-vietnam-war/.

3. Richard Nixon, Address to the Nation Announcing Conclusion of an Agreement on Ending the War and Restoring the Peace in Vietnam, January 23, 1973, in Public Papers of the Presidents of the United States: Richard Nixon, 1973 (Washington DC: Government Printing Office, 1975), 1:20–24.

4. "Vietnamization," History.com. June 7, 2019, https://www.history.com/topics/vietnam-war/vietnamization.

## CHAPTER 4

1. Robert E. Quinn, *Building the Bridge as You Walk on It: A Guide for Leading Change* (San Francisco: Jossey-Bass, 2004), 69–78.

2. The dependence-interdependence road map is based on Covey's Paradigms of Interdependence in Stephen R. Covey, *The 7 Habits of Highly Effective People: Restoring the Character Ethic* (New York: Simon and Schuster, 1989), 48–49.

3. Ben Wigert and Corey Tatel, "The Great Detachment: Why Employees Feel Stuck," Gallup, December 3, 2024, https://www.gallup.com/workplace/653711/great-detachment-why-employees-feel-stuck.aspx.

4. Aesop, "The Four Oxen and the Lion," in *Aesop's Fables*, trans. George Fyler Townsend (London: George Routledge and Sons, 1867).

5. Robert E. Quinn, *Deep Change: Discovering the Leader Within* (San Francisco: Jossey-Bass, 1996).

6. Ruth Wageman, "Interdependence and Group Effectiveness," *Administrative Science Quarterly*, 40, no. 1 (1995): 145–180.

7. Vocabulary.com, s.v. "interdependence," accessed October 5, 2024, https://www.vocabulary.com/dictionary/interdependence.

8. Wonder Lead, "The Human Knot Challenge," YouTube video, 1:24, May 24, 2020, https://www.youtube.com/watch?v=1EIEP0w64s4.

9. Elliott Jaques and Stephen Clement, *Executive Leadership: A Practical Guide to Managing Complexity* (New York: Gordon and Breach Science Publishers, 1991), 4.

10. For additional information on instilling agency, see Paul Napper and Anthony Rao, *The Power of Agency* (New York: St. Martin's Press, 2019).

11. Pierre-Jean Vazel, "Analyzing the Olympic 100-Meter Sprints," HMMR Media, October 8, 2021, https://www.hmmrmedia.com/2021/08/analyzing-the-olympic-100-meter-sprints/.

12. "Michael Phelps Shares Breathtaking Footage of 'One of the Closest Swimming Finishes Ever' in His Swimming Career," *Essentially Sports*, accessed September 8, 2024, https://www.essentiallysports.com/stories/us-sports-news-michael-phelps-shares-breathtaking-footage-of-one-of-the-closest-swimming-finishes-ever-in-his-swimming-career/.

## CHAPTER 6

1. Seth Godin, "The New Craftsmanship," *Seth's Blog*, February 8, 2011, https://seths.blog/2011/02/the-new-craftsmanship/.

2. Monica Moses, "Craft Seriously? What Does the Word Mean?" American Craft Council, March 5, 2020, https://www.craftcouncil.org/magazine/article/craft-seriously-what-does-word-mean#comments.

3. Monica Moses, "Craft Seriously?"

4. *Merriam-Webster,* s.v. "commitment," accessed February 6, 2025, https://www.merriam-webster.com/dictionary/commitment.

5. Robert Hogan, *Personality and the Fate of Organizations* (New York: Lawrence Erlbaum Associates, 2007), 13.

6 . Elliott Jaques and Stephen D. Clement, *Executive Leadership: A Practical Guide to Managing Complexity* (New York: Gordon and Breach Science Publishers, 1991), 4.

7. Hogan, *Personality*, 39.

8. We also recommend the following books to explore the concept of craft, though none directly address leadership as a craft: *Zen and the Art of Motorcycle Maintenance* by Robert M. Pirsig, *On Quality* by Robert M. Pirsig, *Small Is Beautiful* by E. F. Schumacher, *Mastery* by Robert Greene, *Handmade* by Gary Rogowski, *Shop Class as Soulcraft* by Matthew B. Crawford, *Why We Make Things and Why It Matters* by Peter Korn, *The Practice: Shipping Creative Work* by Seth Godin, *Makers: A History of*

*American Studio Craft* by Janet Koplos and Bruce Metcalf, and *The Nature and Art of Workmanship* by David Pye.

## CHAPTER 8

1. William C. Schutz, *The Interpersonal Underworld: A Three-Dimensional Theory of Interpersonal Behavior* (Palo Alto, CA: Science and Behavior Books, 1966).

2. IAPM, "The Iceberg Model," International Association of Project Managers, accessed February 6, 2025, https://www.iapm.net/en/blog/iceberg-model/.

3. "How Much of an Iceberg Is below the Water," Navigation Center, United States Coast Guard, accessed February 6, 2025, https://www.navcen.uscg.gov/how-much-of-an-iceberg-below-the-water.

4. A training group is a group of people under the leadership of a trainer who seek to develop self-awareness and sensitivity to others by verbalizing feelings uninhibitedly at group sessions. An encounter group is an unstructured group that seeks to develop the capacity of the individual to express feelings and to form emotional ties by unrestrained confrontation of individuals.

5. Jeffery J. Kripal, *Esalen: America and the Religion of No Religion* (Chicago: University of Chicago Press, 2007).

6. For more information on the ideas of content and process, see This vs. That, "Content vs. Process: What's the Difference," https://thisvsthat.io/content-vs-process; Center for Growth, "Understanding Process versus Content," https://thecenterforgrowth.com/tips/understanding-process-versus-content; and Six String Soldiers, "Leaving on a Jet Plane [John Denver]," October 20, 2021, YouTube video, 3:43, https://www.youtube.com/watch?v=MUgszQ1wupg.

## CHAPTER 10

1. *Encyclopaedia Britannica*, s.v. "Delphic oracle," last updated June 20, 2025, https://www.britannica.com/topic/Delphic-oracle.

2. *Merriam-Webster*, s.v. "self-awareness," accessed March 24, 2024, https://www.merriam-webster.com/dictionary/self-awareness; Vocabulary.com, s.v., accessed March 24, 2024, "awareness," https://www.vocabulary.com/dictionary/awareness.

3. Leon Moores, "Self-Awareness, the Foundation of Leadership," *Forbes*, February 14, 2024, https://www.forbes.com/sites/forbesbooksauthors/2024/02/14/self-awareness-the-foundation-of-leadership/?sh=2b1c413e4f36.

4. Robert Hogan, *Personality and the Fate of Organizations* (Mahwah, Lawrence Erlbaum Associates, Inc., 2007), viii.

5. Hogan, *Personality and the Fate.*

6. Daniel Goleman, *Emotional Intelligence* (New York: Bantam, 1995).

7. Tasha Eurich, *Insight: The Surprising Truth about How Others See Us, How We See Ourselves, and Why the Answers Matter More Than We Think* (New York: Crown Business, 2017).

8. Korn Ferry Institute, "Korn Ferry Institute Study Shows Link Between Self-Awareness and Company Financial Performance," June 15, 2015 https://www.kornferry.com/about-us/press/korn-ferry-institute-study-shows-link-between-self-awareness-and-company-financial-performance.

9. "Have To Choose To" was an experiential intrapersonal activity that was used as a part of the training at the US Army Organizational Effectiveness Center and School, Fort Ord, California, from 1975 to 1985.

10. American Psychological Association, "Agency," in APA Dictionary of Psychology, last updated April 19, 2018, https://dictionary.apa.org/agency.

11. If you're looking for a starting point for additional sources of information, try one or more of these books, articles, or websites:

- Meir Soloveichik, "25 Years Later, We're All Trapped in 'The Matrix,'" *Wall Street Journal,* March 2024.
- Daniel Goleman, *Emotional Intelligence* (London: Bloomsbury, 1996).
- Emotional Intelligence: Self-Awareness series, *Harvard Business Review*, December 4, 2018.
- Brené Brown, *Dare to Lead* (New York: Random House, 2018).
- Tasha Eurich *Insight* (New York: Crown Business, 2017).
- Michael Carroll, *The Mindful Leader* (Boston: Trumpeter, 2013).

- To understand more about PTSD in veterans, see "PTSD: National Center for PTSD," US Department of Veteran Affairs, https://www.pstd.va.gov; and "PTSD Treatments," American Psychological Association, https://www.apa.org/ptsd-guideline/treatments.
- Bessel van der Kolk, *The Body Keeps Score* (New York: Viking, 2014).
- Andrew B. Brandi, *The Warrior's Guide to Insanity* (Brandi Books, 2007).
- Tasha Eurich, "What Self-Awareness Really Is (and How to Cultivate It)," *Harvard Business Review,* January 4, 2018.
- Paul J. Silva and Maureen E. O'Brien, "Self-Awareness and Constructive Functioning: Revisiting the 'Human Dilemma,'" *Journal of Social and Clinical Psychology* 23, no. 4 (2004): 475–489, https://doi.org/10.1521/jsep.23.23.4.475.40307.
- *Mindfulness meditation*—Apps such as Headspace, Calm, or Insight Timer provide guided meditation practices to cultivate self-awareness and mindfulness.
- *Journaling*—Reflective journaling is a powerful method to gain insight into your thoughts, feelings, and behaviors. Prompts such as "What happened?" "How did I react?" and "What did I learn about myself?" can foster self-awareness.
- *Feedback*—Actively seeking feedback from trusted colleagues, friends, or mentors can reveal blind spots and enhance your understanding of how others perceive you.

12. Buddha, *Dhammapada*, trans. Ānandajoti Bhikkhu, 2nd ed. November 2017, verse 103, 50, https://www.ancient-buddhist-texts.net/Texts-and-Translations/Dhammapada/Dhammapada.pdf.

## CHAPTER 11

1. Daniel Burnett, "Ranger School: My Experience through the Toughest Leadership School in the World," Train Like a Ranger, February 27, 2022, https://www.trainlikearanger.com/post/ranger-school-my-experience-through-the-toughest-leadership-school-in-the-world.

## CHAPTER 12

1. John Uri, "120 Years Ago: The First Powered Flight at Kitty Hawk," NASA, December 14, 2023, https://www.nasa.gov/history/120-years-ago-the-first-powered-flight-at-kitty-hawk/.

2. *Merriam-Webster*, s.v. "information," accessed November 12, 2024, https://www.merriam-webster.com/dictionary/information.

3. *Encyclopaedia Britannica,* s.v. "matter," last updated March 24, 2024, https://www.britannica.com/science/matter.

4. Brooke Sutherland and Ryan Beene, "An Empire Divided," *Bloomberg,* March 20, 2024, https://www.bloomberg.com/features/2024-ge-breakup/.

5. Jona Tarlengco, "What Is a Gemba Walk?" SafetyCulture, January 31, 2024, https://safetyculture.com/topics/gemba-walk/; "Genchi Genbutso," Operations Insider, https://operationsinsider.com/the-language-of-lean/genchi-genbutsu.

6. For more information on the power of language, see Chip Heath and Dan Heath, *Made to Stick: Why Some Ideas Survive and Others Die* (New York: Random House, 2007); and Frank Luntz, *Words That Work: It's Not What You Say, It's What People Hear* (New York: Hyperion, 2007).

## CHAPTER 14

1. Robert F. Mager, *What Every Manager Should Know about Training: An Insider's Guide to Getting Your Money's Worth from Training* (Belmont, CA: Lake Publishing, 1999), 23–24.

2. Bruce Tuckman, "Developmental Sequence in Small Groups," *Psychological Bulletin* 63, no. 6 (1965): 384–399, https://web.mit.edu/curhan/www/docs/Articles/15341_Readings/Group_Dynamics/Tuckman_1965_Developmental_sequence_in_small_groups.pdf; and "Fundamental Interpersonal Relations Orientation," Psychology Concepts, 2020, https://psychologyconcepts.com/fundamental-interpersonal-relations-orientation/.

3. Marcus Aurelius, *Meditations,* trans. Walter J. Black (New York: Walter J. Black, 1945), 20.

4. For more information on team process, see Irvin D. Yalom, *The Theory and Practice of Group Psychotherapy,* 4th ed. (New York: Basic Books, 1995); Shannon Lee, *Be Water My Friend: The Teachings of Bruce Lee* (New York: Flatiron, 2021); Stephanie Wormington, "How to Build Belonging at Work," Center for Creative Leadership, February 21, 2025, https://www.ccl.org/articles/leading-effectively-articles/create-better-culture-build-belonging-at-work/; R. Buckminster Fuller, *Operating Manual for Spaceship Earth* (Switzerland: Lars Müller, 2020); and Jerry Harvey, *The Abilene Paradox* (San Diego, CA: Lexington Books, 1988).

5. Abraham H. Maslow, *The Psychology of Science* (New York: Harper and Row, 1996), 15.

## CHAPTER 16

1. Malcolm S. Knowles, *The Modern Practice of Adult Education: From Pedagogy to Andragogy*, rev. ed. (Chicago: Follett Publishing Company, 1980), 43.

2. Knowles, *The Adult Learner: A Neglected Species* (Houston: Gulf Publishing, 1973), 44.

3. Knowles, *Modern Practice*, 43.

4. William Deresiewicz, "Deep Reading Will Save Your Soul," Persuasion, May 29, 2024, https://www.persuasion.community/p/deep-reading-will-save-your-soul.

5. *State of the Global Workplace Report 2023,* Gallup, 2023, http://www.gallup.com/workplace/349484/state-of-the-global-workplace.aspx.

6. Gallup, Inc. "Employee Engagement," April 14, 2025, https://www.gallup.com/394373/indicator-employee-engagement.aspx.

7. Rick Warren, *The Purpose Driven Life: What on Earth Am I Here For?* (Grand Rapids, MI: Zondervan, 2002), 191.

8. For more information, see John D. Ingalls, *A Trainers Guide to Andragogy: Its Concepts, Experience, and Application* (Washington, DC: US Department of Health, Education, and Welfare, Social and Rehabilitation Service, 1973); Knowles, *Modern Practice*; Jack Mezirow, *Transformative Dimensions of Adult Learning* (San Francisco: Jossey-Bass,

1991); and Stephen D. Brookfield, *The Skillful Teacher: On Technique, Trust, and Responsiveness in the Classroom* (San Francisco: Jossey-Bass, 2006).

## CHAPTER 17

1. Douglas MacArthur, *Reminiscences* (New York: McGraw-Hill, 1964), 82.

## CHAPTER 18

1. Interaction Design Foundation, "What Is Participatory Design?," March 17, 2023, https://www.interaction-design.org/literature/topics/participatory-design.

2. Glenmont Consulting, "Revolutionizing Retail: How Selfridge and Wanamaker Shaped Modern Shopping," November 13, 2023, https://glenmont.co/revolutionizing-retail-how-selfridge-and-wanamaker-shaped-modern-shopping/; and *Encyclopaedia Britannica,* "Harry Gordon Selfridge," April 7, 2024, https://www.britannica.com/money/Harry-Gordon-Selfridge.

3. C. K. Prahalad and Venkat Ramaswamy, *The Future of Competition: Co-Creating Unique Value with Customers* (Boston, MA: Harvard Business School Press, 2004).

4. LEGO Ideas, LEGO, accessed August 24, 2024, https://ideas.lego.com/; Braineet, "My Starbucks Idea: An Open Innovation Success Story," Medium, July 25, 2017, https://medium.com/@Braineet/my-starbucks-idea-an-open-innovation-success-story-13f448ac716c; Nike By You, accessed August 24, 2024, https://www.nike.com/nike-by-you; and Myriam Ertz, "Co-Creation," *Encyclopedia* 4, no. 1 (December 2023): 137–147, https://mdpi.com/2673-839/4/1/12.

5. Johan M. Persson, "Three Great Examples of Co-Creating Companies," C'monde, April 4, 2023, https://www.cmonde.com/3-examples-of-how-co-creation-help-companies-innovate/.

6. Elliott Jaques and Stephen D. Clement, *Executive Leadership: A Practical Guide to Managing Complexity* (New York: Gordon and Breach Science Publishers, 1991), 4.

7. Andy Park, "Brotherhood of the Rope: Reflections on the Relationships between Climbers," *MountainWorld*, May 9, 2007, https://mountainworld.typepad.com/mountainworld/2007/05/brotherhood_of_.html. For more information on mountain climbing and teamwork, see Bernadette McDonald, *The Brotherhood of the Rope: The Biography of Charles Houston* (Seattle: Mountaineers Books, 2007).

8. Jaques and Clement, *Executive Leadership*, 4.

9. Will Guidara, *Unreasonable Hospitality: The Remarkable Power of Giving People More Than They Expect* (New York: Optimism Press, 2022); and Will Guidara, "The Secret Ingredients of Great Hospitality," TED Talk, September 2022, https://www.ted.com/talks/will_guidara_the_secret_ingredients_of_great_hospitality.

## AFTERWORD

1. Ivan Illich, attributed quote, source unconfirmed. The quote is widely cited and aligns with Illich's themes in *Deschooling Society* (New York: Harper and Row, 1971) and *Tools for Conviviality* (New York: Harper and Row, 1973), though no definitive source has been located.

2. Paul Coelho, *The Zahir: A Novel of Obsession* (New York: HarperCollins, 2005), 26.

3. Winston S. Churchill, speech to the House of Commons, October 28, 1943, in Hansard Parliamentary Debates, vol. 393 (London: HMSO, 1943), cols. 403–407.

## APPENDIX B

1. George Land, "TEDx Tucson George Land The Failure of Success," TED Talks, February 16, 2011, YouTube video, 13:06, https://www.youtube.com/watch?v=ZfKMq-rYtnc.

## APPENDIX D

1. Edie West, *The Big Book of Icebreakers: Quick, Fun Activities for Energizing Meetings and Workshops* (New York: McGraw-Hill, 1994).

2. Omagamo, *The Ultimate Icebreaker Playbook: 30 Engaging Games for Corporate, Classroom, Family, and Social Gatherings.* Independently published, 2025.

# Index

# About the Authors

The Co-Creative Leadership Alliance is a multigenerational group of leadership and leadership-development practitioners from around the world. Our informal association spans decades and continents, including Asia Pacific, the Americas, Europe, and the Middle East.

Individually, we've held roles at every level, from first-line manager to C-suite executive, across industries as diverse as consumer goods, retail, hospitality, petroleum, technology, and education. We've worked with frontline workers, union officials, managers, CEOs, business owners, and entrepreneurs, gaining valuable insights from them all.

We think of ourselves as seasoned guides, shaped by years of shared learning. We're grateful to the mentors, colleagues, and communities who have enriched our lives and taught us what it means to lead. Their influence inspired us to embark on the collaborative project of writing this book just before the pandemic in late 2019, with a vision to share our hard-won insights about leadership in today's complex world.

Our book, *Leadership Actually*, is the result of countless conversations, debates, and reflections. Its core message is simple: an organization's success doesn't hinge on its size, technology, or complexity. Instead, it rests on how leadership is perceived and practiced within teams like yours. Leading is a mindset and a set of practical skills informed by the personal sensibilities of leaders and their teams and applied for the benefit of the team, the organization, and each person's own growth.

No single member of our group could have compiled the collective knowledge represented here. Our collaboration reflects our core belief: effective leadership is achieved *together*, not alone, which is the primary reason we chose to write and publish under a group name. To do otherwise would be to undercut everything we believe and teach. Although we didn't agree on everything, we embraced the process, demonstrating the principles this book promotes.

Today, the need for thoughtful, collaborative leadership is greater than ever. As challenges in work and life grow more complex, we as leaders must think critically, communicate effectively, and work together to find innovative solutions. It's our aim that *Leadership Actually* will add to this conversation and continue to spread the message of inclusiveness, agency, collaboration, craft, and co-creation.

We invite you to join us on this journey because, truly, our lives and livelihoods depend on it.